Resources
MANAGEMENT

Titles in the
TEAM LEADER DEVELOPMENT SERIES

Information Management

Sally Palmer

Head of Stockport College of Further and Higher Education Business School.

Margaret Weaver

Lecturer in Business Studies, Stockport College of Further and Higher Education. Fellow of Association of Chartered and Certified Accountants.

Information Management unlocks all the essential communication skills for today's supervisors and team leaders. It includes:

presentation skills from OHPs to video conferencing.
the supervisor's role in team briefings and feedback.
a chapter on how to write a management project.

0 7506 3862 1 : paperback: June 1998

People and Self Management

Sally Palmer

Head of Stockport College of Further and Higher Education Business School.

People and Self Management leads the reader through all the skills needed for today's supervisor/team leader, including:

how to assess and improve your workplace performance.
the essential skills of effective self management.
the management of change.

0 7506 3861 3: paperback: June 1998

Resources Management

Margaret Weaver

Lecturer in Business Studies, Stockport College of Further and Higher Education. Fellow of Association of Chartered and Certified Accountants.

Resources Management is the absolute guide to all areas of resource control. It includes:

● thorough coverage of all areas of resource control for supervisors.
● clear explanations of theories and techniques of control.
● practical exercises to reinforce skills and knowledge.
● application of theory to the work-based problems facing today's managers.

0 7506 3863 X : paperback: June 1998

Activities Management

Cathy Lake

Freelance management writer.

Activities Management is a comprehensive guide to running a smooth and successful operation. It includes:
● practical help on how to plan and manage work.
● health and safety in the workplace.
● environmental considerations that today's supervisor needs to know.
● how to become a quality focussed organization

0 7506 4042 1: paperback: October 1998

Resources
MANAGEMENT

Team Leader Development Series

Margaret Weaver

OXFORD BOSTON JOHANNESBURG MELBOURNE NEW DELHI SINGAPORE

Butterworth-Heinemann
Linacre House, Jordan Hill, Oxford OX2 8DP
225 Wildwood Avenue, Woburn, MA 01801–2041
A division of Reed Educational and Professional Publishing Ltd

℞ A member of the Reed Elsevier plc group

First published 1998

British Library Cataloguing in Publication Data
A catalogue record for this book is available from the British Library

ISBN 0 7506 3863 X

Composition by Genesis Typesetting, Rochester, Kent
Printed and bound in Great Britain

FOR EVERY TITLE THAT WE PUBLISH, BUTTERWORTH-HEINEMANN
WILL PAY FOR BTCV TO PLANT AND CARE FOR A TREE.

Contents

CONTENTS

12 Decision making   181

Feedback   197

Further reading   215

Index   217

Introduction

Introduction

There are four books in the Team Leader Development Series, *People and Self Management*, *Information Management*, *Resources Management* and *Activities Management*, covering key topics from the four principal roles of management. The series has been designed to provide you with the knowledge and skills needed to carry out the role of team leader. The actual name of the job role of a team leader will vary from organization to organization. In your organization, the job role might be called any of the following:

- team leader
- supervisor
- first line manager
- section leader
- junior manager
- chargehand
- foreman
- assistant manager
- administrator.

If you work in the services or a hospital, team leaders may be called by another name not on the above list. However, in this series 'team leader' has been used throughout to describe the job role.

Who the series is intended for

If you have line-management responsibility for people within your organization, or you are hoping to progress to a position in which you will have this responsibility, then this series is for you. You may have been recently promoted into a team leader position or you may have been a team leader for some time. The series is relevant for you whether you work in a small organization or a large organization, whether you work in the public sector, private sector or voluntary sector. The books are designed to provide you with practical help which will enable you to perform better at work and to provide support to a range of programmes of study which have been designed specifically for team leaders.

Related programmes of study

There are a number of management qualifications that have been designed for team leaders. The titles in this series have been structured around the four key roles of management: Managing People, Managing Activities, Managing Resources and Managing Information. The content of each title has been developed in accordance with all the main qualifications in this area. Your tutor, manager or trainer will help you design a programme of study for your particular qualification route. Further details about each syllabus can be found in the tutor supplement that accompanies this textbook.

Resources Management covers the core topics in this key role of management detailed in the programmes of study from the National Examining Board of Supervision and Management, the Institute of Supervisory Management, Edexel and the Institute of Management who all award qualifications in Supervisory Management. The Team Leader Development Series has also been devised to provide material that is relevant for those who are working towards a NVQ or SVQ at level 3 in management. The national management standards at this level cover the full range of general management activities which all managers working in a team leader position are expected to carry out. The Team Leader Development Series covers all the core topics involved with the activities defined in each of the key roles of management listed above. Your tutor will have full details about the national standards.

The content of *Resources Management* covers the essential underpinning knowledge for the following mandatory unit:

B1 Support the efficient use of resources

This unit of competence consists of two elements:

B1.1 Make recommendations for the use of resources
B1.2 Contribute to the control of resources

The work-based assignments, which can be used to gather evidence for your portfolio, are mapped to the relevant elements of competence so that you can see which elements you are working towards.

As part of your work towards a vocational qualification in management at level 3, you also have to demonstrate that you have developed a number of personal competencies (in other words, skills and attitudes) that will enable you to apply your knowledge and understanding to a range of different situations at work. You will cover the range of personal competencies in many aspects of your work. This book will be particularly helpful in providing support for the following personal competencies:

- Communicating
- Focusing on results
- Thinking and taking decisions

Synopsis of *Resources Management*

This textbook looks at the various systems in use to enable resources to be effectively managed. The first chapter gives an overview of different types of organization, their objectives, the environment in which they operate, and the stakeholders who require information on resources. The next four chapters examine the various systems in use for recording, summarizing and managing financial resources, including the most important financial statements and the management of cash. By the end of these chapters, you will understand the need for careful control of cash and other financial resources in an organization. Then follows four chapters which examine how costs are measured, presented and controlled in organizations. There are many different types of cost, which can be treated in different ways according to the information which is required. These chapters emphasize the importance of budgets as a means of control. This area is known as *management accounting,* and is primarily concerned with the provision of internal information for day-to-day decision making. Chapters 10 and 11 look at the documentation and recording methods for other types of resources such as stocks, labour, expenses and fixed assets. The final chapter in the book explores a number of decisions which organizations make in the short term and in the long term, the factors to be considered in making those decisions, and the techniques which can be used to assist management.

Learning structure

Each chapter begins with **Learning objectives**, a list of statements which say what you will be able to do, after you have worked through the chapter. This is followed by the 'Introduction', a few lines which introduce the material that is covered in the chapter.

There are several **Activities** in each chapter. You will find the answers at the end of the book.

There are also **Investigates** in each chapter. These are related to something which has been covered in the text. The suggestion is that you investigate the matter that has just been covered in your own organization. It is important, that you understand what you have learned, but also that you can relate what you have learned to your own organization.

Each chapter has a **Summary**. The summary recaps the main points that have been covered in the chapter. It rounds off the knowledge and skill areas that have been covered in the main body of the chapter, before the text moves into a range of tasks that you can complete to consolidate your learning.

There is a set of **Review and discussion questions** following the summary. You answer these after you have worked through the chapter to check whether you have understood and remembered the information that you have just read. Answers and guidelines to these questions can be found in the tutor resource material.

You are provided with an opportunity to deal with the issues raised in the chapter that you have just read by analysing the **Case study**. The case study is scenario based in the workplace and a chance to 'practise' how you might deal with a situation at work.

There is a **Work-based assignment** at the end of each chapter. These have been designed, so that if you complete the assignment, you will be able to apply the knowledge and skills that you have covered in the chapter in the workplace.

The relevant elements of competence are shown in the portfolio icon where applicable. These will be of use to you if you are studying towards an S/NVQ at Level 3 in management.

1 Organizations and their resources

Learning objectives

On completion of this chapter, you will be able to:

- appreciate the structure of different types of organizations
- understand the nature of different types of business and non-business organizations
- explain the distinction between different methods of business ownership
- appreciate the differing objectives of organizations
- describe the effects of the environment on organizations
- identify the stakeholders in organizations and their information requirements
- appreciate the importance of information systems in providing information to users

Introduction

An organization is a collection of people, things and systems, which work together towards a common set of objectives. In order to achieve those objectives, the various parts of the organization must have individual objectives, and these need to be controlled in order to ensure a successful outcome.

Organizations do not exist in isolation – they react with other organizations and circumstances. It can be said that every organization is a part of a larger organization. For example, a school is an organization which is part of the national educational system; a waste disposal organization is part of the local council, which in turn is part of the system of government of the country.

Organizations need resources in order to operate. The resources needed will vary according to the type of organization and its aims and objectives. An organization that manufactures goods will probably require the entire range of resources, which includes:

- human resources, i.e. people
- physical resources, e.g. buildings, equipment, materials
- financial resources, i.e. money
- services, e.g. energy, information, communication systems

The management of people, information and activities are covered in the complementary texts.

This chapter looks at the different types of organization and their objectives, the environment in which organizations operate, and the resources that they require.

Types of organization and their nature

Formal and informal organizations

A formal organization is one which has a defined structure. This determines responsibilities and levels of authority. Many organizations have 'organization charts' which start with the head of the organization, and work downwards through departmental managers to individual sections.

A 'tall structure' is one with several different levels of authority, each level 'reporting to' the next level up. The structure starts with one person or group of people at the top, and spreads out as it moves down. It can be pictured as a tall triangle as shown in Figure 1.1.

A 'flat structure' is becoming more popular in many organizations, with fewer levels of responsibility (Figure 1.2).

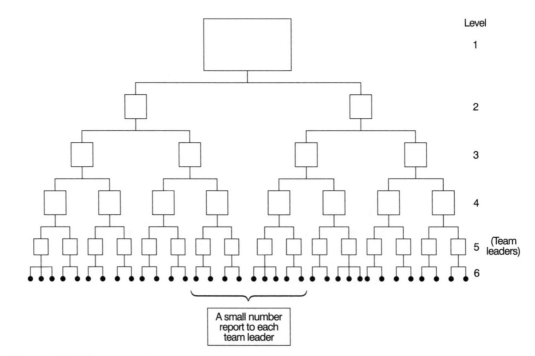

Figure 1.1 Tall organization structure

RESOURCES MANAGEMENT

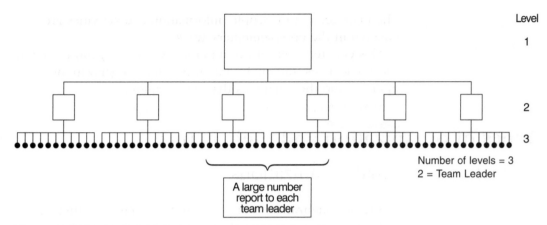

Figure 1.2 Flat organization structure

Other structures exist too, such as the wheel structure illustrated in Figure 1.3. The middle represents a departmental head, with several sections interacting with each other.

Figure 1.4 shows the matrix structure. Each department or team carries out the same functions.

Figure 1.3
Wheel structure

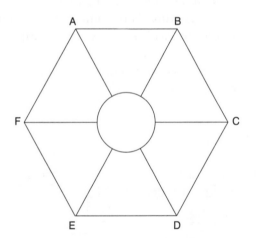

Departments	Functions			
	1	2	3	4
A				
B				
C				
D				
E				
F				

Figure 1.4
Matrix structure

Investigate 1

Obtain or draw for yourself an organization chart for your own organization. Is your organization a 'tall structure', a 'flat structure', or some other structure?

Formal organizations have agreed objectives at all levels, and usually have laid down procedures for operating and ensuring that the objectives are met. Most businesses, in particular large ones, are formal organizations.

Informal organizations are less rigid. Often people assume responsibility for things they are interested in, and reporting is haphazard. Membership of such organizations is voluntary, and sometimes temporary. An example might be a toddler group or a pub quiz team. There is less structure with this type of organization, and although there may be some specific roles allocated to the individuals, e.g. a chairperson, a secretary, a publicity officer, these roles often overlap.

Most organizations have both formal and informal characteristics. A formal organization, such as a hospital, will have laid down objectives, rules, procedures and responsibilities, and decisions will be made at meetings which are properly constructed and minuted. But within the hospital there may be groups of doctors who get together at lunchtime to discuss the latest treatments they have read about in the last month. No agenda or minutes will exist for such an informal meeting.

Business organizations

There are many different types of business organizations. The main types are described here.

Public sector organizations

These are organizations which are run for the benefit of the country, usually by government departments. The number of such organizations has declined dramatically in recent years. Many educational establishments which used to be run by local authorities are now controlled independently, although they do still get some of their funding from the government. Hospitals are another example of organizations which are now self-managed and have to control and justify their costs and revenues.

A few public sector organizations do remain, however, and they are mostly quite large. Examples include the armed forces, the BBC, the Post Office and the Inland Revenue.

They are funded by, and answerable to, the government.

Private sector organizations

The majority of organizations fall into the private sector. The word 'private' can be misleading, as many of these organizations are owned by members of the public. They are not, however owned by the country as a whole.

Manufacturing organizations

Such organizations make and sell goods. The stage of manufacture in which they are involved can vary. A car manufacturer will obtain metal from a sheet metal manufacturer. Tyres will come from a tyre manufacturer, who will have obtained the rubber from a rubber manufacturer. Stationery will have come from a printer, who obtains paper from a paper manufacturer.

Manufacturing used to be the biggest single source of employment in this country, with many people involved in the actual production activities. This has declined in recent years as a result of cheaper and better quality imports and the use of modern technology. Only about twenty per cent of all workers are in the manufacturing sector nowadays.

Trading organizations

These buy in goods already made and sell them on to other organizations or to the public. An example is a dealer in electrical goods.

Service organizations

The number of service organizations is growing, both large and small. The sector includes hospitals, accountants, solicitors, hairdressers, plumbers, schools, shops, banks and insurance companies.

Voluntary organizations

These too are growing in number and the range of services they provide, perhaps due to the increasing need which people have for support, and the lack of funds from the government. They rely heavily on donations of money from the public, and most of them have 'charitable status' which enables them to obtain certain tax exemptions.

Examples include organizations that deal with the elderly, disabled, children, animals, the environment and human rights. Many of them are staffed by volunteers who might be paid only for their travelling costs. However, the larger voluntary organizations do have formal management structures and procedures to ensure their continued survival and to provide reassurance to the public that they are utilizing their resources effectively.

Business ownership

The sole trader

A sole trader is a person who owns the whole of the business. He or she provides the bulk of the funds to set up and run the business, and takes all the risks and rewards of ownership. The business may employ people, so they are not necessarily one-person businesses. They are, however, mostly small businesses, and account for around ninety per cent of all businesses in the country. Some sole traders remain small, others grow and need to consider taking on one or more partners, or even converting to a limited company.

The sole trader has what is called 'unlimited liability' for the debts of the business. This means that if the business owes money which it cannot repay, the belongings of the owner can be seized in order to pay those debts.

The partnership

This exists where there are two or more owners. They share the responsibility of providing the funds, and divide out the profits between them in an agreed manner - not necessarily equally. A partnership often develops where the owners have different skills to offer to the business, or where there is a need for more money than a sole trader can provide.

Partners also have unlimited liability as with sole traders, except that there is the opportunity for some partners to limit their liability providing that they do not take part in the running of the business.

Most partnerships are fairly small, although some very large businesses started off as partnerships and continued to grow very rapidly while still remaining as partnerships.

The limited company

A limited company is one where the owners have 'limited liability' for the debts of the organization. The funds invested in the organization are divided into 'shares', and each owner buys some of the shares for an agreed price to provide the capital which the business requires. Each owner's liability is limited to the agreed price of shares, and if they have already paid that, there is no further liability.

The Conservative government prior to 1997 set out to encourage share ownership and many organizations such as building societies and insurance providers became companies, with the result that many people who had previously never owned shares became shareholders in those companies. Because of the 'limited liability' of such companies, in the event that the company is unable to pay its debts, the maximum amount that the shareholders can lose is their shares in the business. They will not be called upon to pay any more.

Shareholders receive a share of the profits by being paid 'dividends'. A dividend is usually calculated at a number of pence per share, or as a percentage of the share price. Often only part of the profits are paid out as dividends, with the rest being kept in the business for future use.

The public limited company

This type of limited company can sell its shares to anyone. They have the letters 'plc' after their name, and may trade their shares on the stock exchange, although not all do so. The majority of 'famous name' companies are plcs.

ORGANIZATIONS AND THEIR RESOURCES

The private limited company

This type of limited company is only able to sell its shares by agreement with the other shareholders. They are often family businesses who want the security of limited liability, but who do not want ownership of the company to pass to outsiders.

Again, there are some fairly large companies that are private.

Organizational objectives

Whether formal or informal, all organizations have objectives, even though these might not be stated so clearly. In informal organizations, the objectives often develop as time passes and may change frequently.

For most businesses, the chief objective is financial – to make a profit and remain solvent. You will see later in this book that both these objectives are important, and are not necessarily the same as each other. If sufficient profit is made, the organization has the funds to grow; if it is solvent it is able to pay its way.

Many other objectives exist instead of or alongside the financial objectives. A nursing home's objectives will include the provision of high-quality care to its patients. This might even be its main objective, with profit being less important.

Other objectives might include things such as:

- to increase market share by ten per cent
- to develop new products
- to reduce staff turnover
- to achieve the Investors in People award

Some of these objectives will be determined by top management. These are 'strategic objectives' and are often published. Middle managers will have 'tactical objectives' which support the strategic ones, and junior management and team leaders will have 'operational objectives' which govern the day-to-day work. The companion text entitled Managing Information explains these levels of management in more detail.

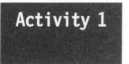

List six strategic objectives which might exist in a sports centre.

See Feedback section for answer to this activity.

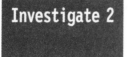

Obtain a copy of your organization's strategic objectives. Did you know they existed? What are your own objectives? Do they contribute towards the achievement of your organization's objectives?

The operating environment

Open and closed systems

No organization exists entirely on its own. It relies on other organizations and contributes itself to other organizations. It is affected by the situation outside as much as inside. This is its 'environment'.

The human-being could be likened to an organization. It is a system of interconnected parts which work together to achieve common objectives – usually to live, to enjoy that life, to earn a good salary, and so on. But it cannot do this by itself. It needs food from the supermarket, work outside the home, holidays, electricity, education. It also reacts to the environment, for example by feeling cold or hot.

Each organization has a 'boundary' which contains it. The human-being's boundary is its skin. But it also has an external environment outside that boundary. This is known as an 'open system' – one which reacts with its environment. Most systems are open systems. Closed systems are hard to imagine, except perhaps completely isolated scientific experiments.

External influences on organizations

If an organization is an open system, then you need to look at some of the influences on it which come from outside, because these will affect many of the things which the organization does. These external influences include the following:

- economic influences – inflation rates or the level of unemployment
- financial influences – interest rates, foreign exchange rates, taxation rates
- political influences – policies on imports and exports, training targets
- social influences – reduced working hours, increased holiday periods, flexible working
- ecological influences – pressures for reduced pollution, the use of natural materials
- market influences – consumer tastes and trends, competitors' activities
- technological influences – new discoveries, the use of computers, new manufacturing methods
- legal influences – regarding product safety, employment laws, health and safety legislation

Many of these will have an impact on the way in which organizations work. Some will be of assistance, others will be expensive or even detrimental. Larger organizations will be affected by all of these, because they are more complex than small ones.

List the eight external influences which might affect an organization's operations.

Refer to the list above to check your list.

Stakeholders in organizations

Many people have an interest or 'stake' in an organization. These are the people who need to know how the organization has performed, and will perform in the future. They need to have access to various types of information according to their needs. The major stakeholders, and their need for information can be shown in Table 1.1.

Much of the information in Table 1.1 is financial, but all the resources of an organization contribute towards providing information to those who require it.

Table 1.1 Major stakeholders and organizations

Stakeholder	Information needed	Use of information
Managers	Costs, revenues, cash flow, profitability of individual products – materials, labour and overhead costs; internal and external factors	Decision making – new products, abandoning products, working methods
Owners	Profitability, stability, share prices	Investment decisions
Lenders	Cash balances; assets; other debts; profits	To decide whether to lend; to ensure interest payments are met
Employees	Profits; cash; future plans; labour costs; labour turnover rates	To assess job security; future ability to pay wages and pensions
Customers	Profits; reliability; availability of materials and finished products	To ensure supply of good quality goods
Government	Profits; statistics	To determine tax liabilities; to provide national statistics
The public	Objectives; operating methods; future plans	To determine the impact of activities on the community

Information systems in organizations

The book entitled *Information Management* gives detailed descriptions of information systems in organizations.

Internal information systems cover the operations of the organization, with details of stocks, production methods and costs, labour rates and efficiency, energy usage, overhead costs, budgets, the condition of equipment, and so on. The information is used to make everyday and periodic decisions. The data comes from within the organization and is used within the organization.

External information systems include public databases, such as marketing information, government statistics, economic trends, etc.

Past, present and future resources

Organizations use information from the past to determine their present performance standards. These might be measured against the performance of other organizations.

All of this information is used to determine the need for future resources.

ORGANIZATIONS AND THEIR RESOURCES

Summary

Now that you have completed this chapter you should understand how different organizations are structured, and appreciate the different types of structure. You should appreciate the different types of organization and their ownership. Organizations have a variety of objectives and the environment in which they operate will affect their achievement of those objectives. You should understand the many types of information needed by the stakeholders in organizations and how it is used by them.

Review and discussion questions

1 What is an organization composed of?
2 What is the difference between a formal and an informal organization?
3 List six different types of business organization
4 Briefly describe the three categories of business ownership and discuss their differences
5 List eight external influences on organizations
6 Identify seven groups of stakeholder and the types of information they need

Case study

Peter is thinking of starting a business. He has been working for an employer for the past ten years and feels that it is time that he 'did his own thing'. He does not enjoy having to answer to other people for his actions, and thinks that if he is in charge of his own business he will be able to get on with the job without any interference from anyone else.

The manufacturing business he plans to start is in an expanding field, and he envisages it becoming quite sizeable very quickly.

Peter has no experience of running a business. He knows little about the way in which businesses operate, and he has asked your advice.

Write a short report to Peter outlining the different aspects of business organization which he will need to consider in the running of his business.

RESOURCES MANAGEMENT

**Work-based
assignment**

Look at your own organization. Make brief notes on each of
the following points as they affect your organization:

- the structure of your organization
- the type of organization
- its owners
- its strategic objectives
- the operational objectives which affect your own work
- the external influences on your organization
- its major stakeholders

2 Financial accounts

Learning objectives

On completion of this chapter you will be able to:

- understand what is meant by 'accounting' and why it is important
- explain the difference between book-keeping, financial accounting and management accounting
- understand the need for financial statements
- explain the main terms used in financial statements
- understand the purpose of the three main financial statements
- prepare simple financial statements for a sole trader and a limited company
- understand the difference between cash and profit
- appreciate the need for control and regulation in accounting

Introduction

This chapter outlines the different aspects of accounting, and in particular looks at the main financial statements which organizations prepare. It introduces several accounting terms which will help you to understand some of the jargon used by accountants. While it is unlikely that you will be responsible for the preparation of financial statements unless you are employed in an accounting environment, there may be occasions when the work you do contributes to their preparation, or where you need to discuss financial matters with accountants.

The chapter also explains the very important difference between cash and profit – the two most misunderstood and probably the most important areas of accounting.

What is 'accounting'?

Accounting is concerned with providing information for control, planning and decision making by its users. In Chapter 1 you looked at the different uses of accounting information, by the 'stakeholders' in an organization. This information is provided to the stakeholders in a variety of ways. Some is provided by the organization itself, some by the government, and some by other bodies such as the Institute of Management, the trade unions, and financial advisers.

Much accounting information orginates from the measurement of various values placed on the transactions which occur in the organization. Measurements are required in many different situations, for example:

- to determine quantities of goods in stock, or goods needing to be ordered
- to calculate levels of insurance cover
- to anticipate cash excesses and shortages
- to calculate wages
- to determine the cost of goods and services
- to determine selling prices
- to calculate amounts to be paid to suppliers
- to indicate the success and stability of the organization
- to calculate tax liabilities
- to assess the risk involved in new ventures

The Chartered Institute of Management Accounting (CIMA) defines accounting as:

- the classification and recording of monetary transactions
- the presentation and interpretation of the results of those transactions in order to assess performance over a period and the financial position at a given date, and
- the monetary projection of future activities arising from alternative planned courses of action

Although this definition of accounting is widely accepted, it tends to concentrate on 'monetary' transactions. Not all aspects of organizations are concerned entirely with monetary transactions. A team leader in a supermarket might be more interested in the number of customers waiting at the checkout at any one time; a team leader on a hospital ward might be concerned about the number of patients to be admitted next week. The definition could be extended to include a fourth objective, such as:

- the identification and measurement of quantitative and economic information to aid planning, control and decision making by managers

These four elements of the definition cover the whole of the accounting function.

Book-keeping

Book-keeping is the recording of monetary transactions in sufficient detail to enable its accuracy to be checked, and in such a way that relevant summarized information can be extracted from the book-keeping records to satisfy the other two areas of accounting.

This text does not cover the book-keeping function of an organization, except for an introduction for the need to maintain adequate records of cash and bank transactions, and how to use the information provided by the book-keeping system for other purposes.

The 'books of account' are called *ledgers*. The word 'account' means 'a record of'. Thus, a 'Motor Expenses account' will contain a record of all the transactions involving motor expenses. It might go back for several years. In most organizations, accounts are held on computer nowadays, and are split into different sections for the different categories of accounts. The following ledgers are commonly found in organizations:

- a sales ledger, which contains accounts for customers (also called *debtors*)
- a purchase ledger, which contains accounts for suppliers (also called *creditors*)
- a cash book, which contains bank accounts and cash accounts
- a general or 'nominal' ledger which contains all the other accounts

The general ledger contains a wide variety of accounts. Many of these will be mentioned throughout this chapter.

The ledgers are summarized periodically. This summary is called a 'trial balance', and it contains a list of all the ledger accounts and their final position or 'balance'.

Financial accounting

This follows on from the book-keeping system, and is intended to present summarized information on the monetary transactions. It is provided to both internal and external users of information, but the method of presentation and the level of detail will be different for both groups.

Information provided to external users is primarily in the form of financial statements, mainly the profit and loss account, the balance sheet and the cash flow statement. In most limited companies, these statements are required to be prepared by law, and their format is laid down in the Companies Acts. In other types of business, these statements can be prepared to suit the users, who may be mainly internal users, and their format depends on their requirements. A small sole trader, for example, is not required to produce any financial accounts at all, but does need to keep records in order to report the annual profit to the Inland Revenue. Larger sole traders do need to prepare some financial statements for the Inland Revenue, and to supply details of value added tax (VAT) to HM Customs and Excise, but these statements can be in any form to suit the individual as long as they provide the required information.

In a small business, the owners and managers probably need access to *all* the financial information, but this is not the case in larger businesses. It is interesting to know how much profit a large organization has made during a year, but it is more important to know how your own section contributed towards that. Financial accounts do not normally break results down into sections. They are highly summarized.

Financial accounts are also mostly concerned with reporting past activities. While this is often useful, most managers want information about the present and the future in order to do their jobs effectively.

Finally, financial accounts are usually produced only annually, or perhaps half-yearly. Imagine being in charge of your team and only reviewing their results once a year!

Investigate 3

Obtain the financial accounts for your organization, or one in which you are interested. If your organization is a public limited company, these are often available to employees, or the 'annual report' can be obtained from the company's registered office. If your organization is a smaller one, you can get copies of plcs' accounts by ringing the telephone number given in the *Financial Times* or other newspapers.

Look at the financial information provided in the annual report and accounts. The financial statements often cover only a few pages of the report, with the rest being taken up by background information about the company.

If you were a manager, or team leader, in a company like this, would the information given be of much use to you? What additional information would be useful to you?

Management accounting

This area of accounting is intended to provide managers at all levels within the organization, with the information they need to enable them to plan, control and make decisions. The information provided in management accounting systems is largely internal and highly detailed. It is also provided at regular intervals throughout the year, perhaps monthly, or even weekly or daily. It is not usually available to 'outsiders' and some of it is even confidential. It is, nevertheless, very important as a tool to enable managers to do their jobs.

Management accounting systems do not provide just monetary information, but might include information on:

- number of hours worked by employees
- quantities produced
- number of outstanding orders
- customers who have not paid
- maintenance records for machinery
- number of machine stoppages due to faulty materials
- customer complaints

and so on. Much of this information would never be disclosed to the public.

Investigate 4

Identify the internal information which you produce in your job. Is any of it available to people outside the organization?

Financial statements for sole traders

The three main financial statements which an organization produces are:

- the profit and loss account
- the balance sheet
- the cash flow statement

All of these are produced mainly for external use, for they are often in insufficient detail to be used by internal management.

Unless you are employed in an accounting environment, you are unlikely to have to prepared these statements yourself, but you might be required to use them and understand them.

The profit and loss account of a sole trader

This statement brings together the *revenues earned* and the *expenses consumed in earning that revenue.* It is normally prepared for a period covering a year, although some organizations prepare them more often.

Revenues earned

This is money earned from the ordinary day-to-day activities of the organization. It includes items such as sales revenue, commissions, fees, interest from invesments, rental income and so on. Revenue from sales is often called 'turnover'.

It is important to understand the difference between revenues *earned* and revenues *received*. Revenue is earned when the contract to supply the goods and services has been completed and the customer is legally obliged to pay. This is different from actually receiving the money, which could be several months later. As soon as the revenue is earned, it forms part of the profit which the organization has made.

So, all the goods sold during a year will make up the revenue for the year, even if some have yet to be paid for. Those customers who still owe money at the end of the year are called *debtors*. Section 4 will explain what happens to these in more detail.

Expenses consumed in earning revenue

Expenses are consumed as soon as they are used up. As with revenue, the fact that some might not have been paid for is irrelevant. It is their usage which determines whether they should be included as expenses for the year.

Examples include the cost of goods which have been sold, stationery used, telephone calls made, heat and light used up, wages earned by employees, annual rental charges, interest payable on loans, and so on.

Suppliers of goods and services whose invoices are still to be paid at the end of the year are called *creditors*. Some

FINANCIAL ACCOUNTS

suppliers may not have sent in their invoices by the end of the year – for example, your year end might be 31 December, but the quarterly gas bill is not due until after the end of January. When it comes, it will include gas consumed during November and December. This needs to be estimated and included as expenses consumed during the year. The estimate is called an *accrued expense*. Section 4 will also explain what happens to creditors and accrued expenses.

Sometimes an organization has to pay in advance for some goods and services. For example, your annual insurance premium might be paid on 1 July each year, covering the period to 30 June in the following year. By 31 December you will have used only half of the premium, with the remainder having been paid in advance for the following half year. Only the half used up will be included as an expense for the year to 31 December; the other half is called a *prepaid expense*. Section 4 will also explain what happens to prepaid expenses.

Depreciation

An organization will probably spend money on items of equipment, motor vehicles, etc. which are still in existence at the end of the year, and will be used in the following year. As these have not been used up during the year, they are not expenses consumed. However, most of these items do wear out over time, or lose value. This is known as *depreciation*. The amount which it is estimated these items have fallen in value, or the value placed on the amount of wear during the year, is an expense, and is included in the calculation of profit.

The amount is often estimated by simply taking the cost of the item (less any expected value from its sale in the future) and dividing it by the number of years it is expected to be in use. There are other methods of depreciation, but this method is the simplest to operate. It is called *straight line depreciation,* because the amount used does not vary from year to year.

Wages and drawings

The wages to be included as expenses are those paid to employees. Any amounts taken by the owner are called 'drawings' and should not be included as expenses.

A sample profit and loss account for a solicitor

A.G. Green, Profit and loss account for the year ended 31 December xxx1

	£	£
Fees earned		50,000
Less expenses		
Secretary's wages	8,000	
Insurance	4,000	
Heat and light	1,000	
Stationery	2,000	
Telephone	1,500	
Rent and rates	1,200	
Depreciation of equipment	500	
		18,200
Net profit		31,800

'Net' profit is the profit after all expenses have been deducted from the revenue.

The solicitor might still be owed £5,000 of the fees (debtors), but nevertheless they are included in the above total. She might still owe £200 for the telephone bill, which has not yet been received (an accrued expense), and £500 for a stationery bill which is unpaid (a creditor). The equipment might have cost £2,500 at the beginning of the year, and is expected to last for five years, with no value at the end.

The trading account

Some organizations are involved in *trading*, which means that they buy (or make) and sell goods rather than performing services. These organizations usually calculate profit in two stages:

1 Gross profit is the revenue earned from sales, less the cost to the organization of the goods which have been sold.
2 Net profit is the gross profit, less all other expenses

Gross profit is calculated in the *trading account*. Note that it only includes the cost of the goods which have been sold. This means the cost of making them, or buying them in. It does not include the cost of selling them, delivering them to customers or any other expenses.

Opening and closing stocks

As it is only expenses which have been consumed during the year which go towards calculating profit, it is important to realize that expenditure on things which are not used up is excluded. So, you would not include the cost of goods which are still in stock at the end of the year.

It is likely that the organization will have stocks of goods or materials at the beginning and end of the year, as well as goods and materials bought during the year. These need to be considered carefully when working out the cost of those which have been sold. The stocks at the beginning (opening stocks) need to be added to those bought during the year (purchases), and any stocks at the end (closing stocks) need to be deducted. This then gives a figure of 'Cost of goods sold' or 'Cost of sales'. This is the expense 'consumed' during the year.

Example

At the beginning of xxx1, Jane has a stock of goods for sale which cost £4,000. During the year they buy in more goods costing £24,000, and at the end of the year they still have stocks remaining which cost £3,000.

Cost of goods sold:	£
Opening stocks	4,000
Purchases	24,000
	28,000
Less Closing stocks	3,000
	25,000

£25,000 is the cost of the goods which have been sold during the year. If they were sold for £45,000, then gross profit is £20,000 (£45,000 − £25,000).

Activity 3

Calculate the cost of goods sold by Lesley Biggs, if opening stocks are £14,000, purchases are £120,000 and closing stocks are £12,000.

See Feedback section for answer to this activity.

The trading and profit and loss accounts are usually combined into one account. So, for Jane, the account might be as follows:

Jane – Trading and profit and loss account for the year ending 31 December xxx1

	£	£
Sales		45,000
Less Cost of goods sold:		
Opening stocks	4,000	
Purchases	24,000	
	28,000	
Less Closing stocks	3,000	
		25,000
GROSS PROFIT		20,000
Less Expenses:		
Wages and salaries	2,200	
Selling costs	800	
Administration costs	3,000	
Depreciation	2,000	
		8,000
NET PROFIT		12,000

In a sole trader's business, the whole of the profit belongs to the owner, so there is no need to do anything further with the net profit except to add it to the owner's investment in the business. Of course, a business can also make a net loss, which is deducted from the owner's investment.

Activity 4

Using the cost of goods sold from Activity 3 (you should have arrived at £122,000) prepare the trading and profit and loss account for Lesley Biggs, from the following information:

Sales £180,000, Motor expenses £18,000, Printing, post and stationery £5,000, Wages and salaries £24,000. In addition there is a motor vehicle which cost £10,000 and is expected to last for five years.

See Feedback section for answer to this activity.

The balance sheet of a sole trader

The balance sheet is a statement of the position of the business at a particular point in time – usually just after the profit has been calculated. It is sometimes called a 'snapshot' of the organization. Unlike the profit and loss account, which shows what has been taking place over a period of time, the balance sheet shows how the business stands now.

It contains the assets and liabilities which the organization has at that point, and the investment in the business by the owners.

Assets

Assets are things which an organization possesses. There are two main categories:

- Fixed assets are those which are intended to be used for a long period of time. Examples include land, buildings, equipment, furniture, motor vehicles.
- Current assets are those which are intended to be used for only a short period of time, or which change frequently. Examples include stocks of materials and goods, stocks of stationery, bank and cash balances, debtors and prepaid expenses.

Debtors are people who owe money to the business, usually because they have bought goods 'on credit', which means they do not pay at once. You have already learnt that once the goods have been sold they are included in the sales revenue in the profit and loss account, whether paid for or not. But when the balance sheet is drawn up, any amounts still owing will be part of the 'snapshot' of the organization at that time. Although the organization does not yet have this money, it is still an asset because it belongs to the organization.

Prepaid expenses are expenses which have already been paid, but their value has not yet been used up. The business has the benefit of them still to come, thus they are assets.

Liabilities

Liabilities are amounts owed by the organization to people who have provided it with money, goods or services, and have yet to be repaid. There are two main categories:

- Long-term liabilities are those which are to be repaid after more than a year. Examples include mortgages, loans, hire purchase commitments.
- Current liabilities are those which are to be repaid within the next year. Examples include creditors for goods and services, bank overdrafts, accrued expenses.

Bank overdrafts are always regarded as current liabilities even in those organizations who use them for years and years, because in theory a bank overdraft can be called in for repayment immediately.

Accrued expenses includes any amount which the organization owes for expenses already consumed but for which a bill has not yet been received. An example would be gas consumed during the previous year but where the bill is not yet due. Accrued expenses are often estimated.

Capital

Capital is the money put into or left in the organization by its owner. In a sole trader's business this will include the original investment and any previous profits left in the business, plus the profit made during the year just ended, less any amounts drawn out.

The accounting equation

The assets less the liabilities is said to represent the 'net worth of the business' – in other words, its value to the owner. The accounting equation shows this as:

> Assets minus liabilities = owner's capital

Example

Jane has the following assets and liabilities at 31 December xxx1:

	£
Fixed assets	18,000
Current assets	11,000
Total assets	29,000
Long-term liabilities	10,000
Current liabilities	6,000
Total liabilities	16,000

So, Jane's capital must be £13,000 (£29,000 − £16,000).

This might be financed as follows:

	£
Capital at 1 January xxx1	8,000
Profit during xxx1	12,000
	20,000
less drawings during xxx1	7,000
Capital at 31 December xxx1	13,000

These figures will form Jane's balance sheet at 31 December xxx1.

Activity 5

(a) What is the capital for a business which has £120,000 in assets and £90,000 in liabilities?
(b) If a business has £40,000 of capital and £20,000 of liabilities, what are its assets?

See Feedback section for answer to this activity.

Working capital

The above example shows the total of assets, less the total of liabilities, to equal capital. It does not show a very important figure to most businesses – how much of that capital is available to 'work' with on a day-to-day basis. If the business needs to spend, say, £8,000 in the next month, does it have that amount of money available? From the figures above it looks as if it has £13,000 available. But some of this is 'tied up' in fixed assets – a business does not normally want to sell these in order to raise money. And some of the liabilities are not due for repayment for a long time. The amount which is likely to be available in the near future is calculated from the *current* assets and liabilities.

The current assets are those which are either already cash, or are likely to be turned into cash in the near future. The current liabilities are those which will need to be paid out of those assets. The remainder is the 'working capital' of the organization. It is also known as 'net current assets'.

So, for Jane, working capital is:

Current assets	£11,000	
less current liabilities	£ 6,000	
Working capital		£5,000

This shows that Jane does not have enough to spend £8,000 next month.

Now have a look at Jane's balance sheet, showing the working capital:

Jane – Balance sheet at 31 December xxx1

	£	£
Fixed assets		18,000
Current assets	11,000	
less Current liabilities	6,000	
Working capital		5,000
		23,000
less Long-term liabilities		10,000
		13,000
Financed by:		
Capital at 1 January xxx1		8,000
Profit during xxx1		12,000
		20,000
less Drawings during xxx1		7,000
Capital at 31 December xxx1		13,000

Note that the two figures which are 'double underlined' are the same. If this is not the case, something has gone wrong!

A point about asset values

You were told in the above paragraph that assets minus liabilities equal the 'net worth' of the business. This is assuming that the assets are worth the figures given. In many cases this will not be true.

Fixed assets usually decrease in value over time (depreciate). The depreciation each year is deducted from the original cost, and the figure shown on the balance sheet is called the 'net book value', i.e. the value according to the books of the business. As depreciation is estimated, then the values shown in the balance sheet may not reflect the true value. Some assets even increase in value, and this may or may not be shown on the balance sheet.

Debtors are customers who owe money to the business. Some of these may not pay up, so the figure may not truly represent what is likely to be received.

Stocks are usually valued at their cost of purchase. They may be worth less than this, because they are out of date or out of fashion. Or they may be worth more if they can be sold for a higher figure.

If the business were to be sold as a 'going concern' (a thriving business), it might sell for much more than the net worth as shown in the balance sheet.

So, balance sheet values cannot always be relied upon to give a true picture of the worth of the business. This should always be borne in mind when looking at the financial accounts.

A detailed balance sheet

Jane's balance sheet earlier is very simple, and gives no breakdown of individual assets and liabilities, so it is not very useful to its users. A more detailed version might be as shown on page 29.

Activity 6

Your answer to Activity 4 should have been £9,000 net profit for Lesley Biggs.

You have the following additional information:

Customers who still owed money at the end of xxx1 amounted to £23,000, and suppliers who were still unpaid were £8,000. Motor expenses prepaid were £500, and printing costs outstanding were £300. The balance at the bank was £10,000. Lesley's capital at the start of the year was £46,000, and she withdrew £14,800 for herself during the year. She also had a long-term bank loan of £5,000.

Prepare her balance sheet at 31 December xxx1.

Jane – Balance sheet at 31 December xxx1

	£	£	£
Fixed assets			
Machinery – costs		20,000	
– depreciation		2,000	
			18,000
Current assets			
Stocks	3,000		
Debtors	5,000		
Prepaid expenses	500		
Cash and bank	2,500		
		11,000	
less Current liabilities			
Creditors	5,700		
Accrued expenses	300		
		6,000	
Working capital			5,000
			23,000
less Long-term liabilities			
loan			10,000
			13,000
Financed by:			
Capital at 1 January xxx1			8,000
Profit during xxx1			12,000
			20,000
less Drawings during xxx1			7,000
Capital at 31 December xxx1			13,000

The cash flow statement

Did you notice that although Jane made a net profit of £12,000 during xxx1, she had only £2,500 in the bank? Suppose that last year she had £3,000. Can you think why the bank balance has gone down, even though she made a profit?

Well, for a start, she withdrew £7,000 of that profit as drawings. And the profit and loss account contains depreciation of £2,000 which is nothing to do with cash at all. Money is spent when fixed assets are bought, and depreciation is just an adjustment to the value – no money changes hands at that point. In addition, the profit and loss account contains the total of goods sold – and we know that not all customers have paid up yet; there will also have been money received during the year from *last year's* customers who didn't pay until this year. And the same will apply to Jane's suppliers – not all have been paid during the year.

Other things might have happened to affect cash. She might have bought extra fixed assets during the year, or repaid part of the loan. Transactions such as these have no effect on the profit, but they certainly affect the bank balance.

There are many different ways of comparing the profit with the change in cash and bank balances. Limited companies are required to prepare a statement, called a cash flow statement in a strict format. At this stage in your studies, you will not be expected to know that format. It is sufficient that you understand that not everything in the profit and loss account involves cash, and some things affect cash without affecting profit. Yet others, like sales, affect both cash and profit, but not at the same time.

The easiest way of drawing up a cash flow statement is to adjust the net profit for items such as depreciation, which do not affect cash, and then to compare the changes in the balance sheet from last year to this year.

Here are Jane's balance sheets for the years xxx0 and xxx1, with the changes noted:

Jane – Balance sheets at 31 December

	xxx1 £	xxx0 £	Change £
Fixed assets			
Machinery – cost	20,000	4,000	+16,000
depreciation	3,000	1,000	+2,000
	17,000	3,000	
Current assets			
Stocks	3,000	4,000	–1,000
Debtors	5,000	2,800	+2,200
Prepaid expenses	500	500	
Cash and bank	2,500	3,000	–500
	11,000	10,300	
less Current liabilities			
Creditors	5,700	5,000	+700
Accrued expenses	300	300	
	6,000	5,300	
Working capital	5,000	5,000	
	22,000	8,000	
less Long-term loan	9,000	nil	+9,000
	13,000	8,000	

Financed by:

Capital at 1 January	8,000	9,000
Profit during the year	12,000	15,000
	20,000	24,000
less Drawings during	7,000	16,000
Capital at 31 December	13,000	8,000

Cash inflows

Some of the changes mean that cash has flowed in during the year. Cash flows in for many reasons, such as:

• making a profit
• selling fixed assets
• obtaining a loan
• reducing debtors (which means that more have paid up)
• reducing stocks (which means less has been bought)
• increasing creditors (which means fewer have been paid)

Cash outflows

Some changes mean that cash has flowed out. These include:

• buying fixed assets
• repaying loans
• increasing debtors
• increasing stocks
• decreasing creditors
• owner's drawings

We can now prepare the cash flow statement. This version starts with the profit, adjusted for depreciation, and ends with the change in the bank balance:

Jane – cash flow statement for xxx1

Net profit	12,000	
Add back depreciation	2,000	
Cash flow from operations		14,000
Cash inflows		
Decrease in stocks	1,000	
Increase in creditors	700	
Increase in loan	9,000	
		10,700
		24,700

FINANCIAL ACCOUNTS

Cash outflows

Drawings	7,000	
Purchase of fixed assets	16,000	
Increase in debtors	2,200	
		25,200
Net cash outflow during the year		500
Bank balance at beginning		3,000
Bank balance at end		2,500
Net decrease in bank balance		500

Activity 7

Which of the following result in cash flows in and which in cash flows out?

- an increase in debtors
- a loss
- a decrease in creditors
- an increase in stocks
- the purchase of fixed assets
- the repayment of a loan
- the sale of fixed assets
- owner's drawings

See Feedback section for answer to this activity.

Financial accounts for limited companies

Many of the items which appear in the accounts of sole traders also appear in the accounts of limited companies. However, there are some special items in limited company accounts.

Share capital

Chapter 1 mentioned that limited companies raise their capital by splitting their requirements into a number of shares, and investors purchase these. Each share has a *par value*, also called the nominal or face value. A company might be authorized to issue 1 million shares with a par value of £1.

When it issues shares to investors, it might issue them for more than £1 – because investors might be prepared to pay more. So if it wants to raise £1 million, it could issue all its shares at par, or it could issue say 250,000 shares and charge £4 each for them. This difference between the *issue price* and the *par value* is called the 'share premium'. It then has the possibility of raising further capital in the future by issuing some of the remaining 750,000 shares.

The shareholders are owners of the company. The proportion which they own depends on the type of shares – there are several different types. In this book, you will deal only with *Ordinary shares*, which are the most common.

Once the owners have their shares, they can sell them to other people for any price they can get. This is a private deal between the individuals and the company concerned does not directly benefit from it. The price that they can be sold for is called the *market value*. This is the figure you see quoted in the newspapers.

Dividends

These too were mentioned in Chapter 1. Shareholders are paid a proportion of the profits as dividends, usually quoted in pence per share. It does not matter how much the shareholders paid for their shares – they get the same amount per share. Dividends are the equivalent of drawings in a sole trader's accounts. They are not expenses.

The directors decide whether or not a dividend is to be 'declared'. They may decide to keep all the profits in the business and not pay dividends, or they may decide to make a large payout. This is a risk that ordinary shareholders take.

A company cannot pay out dividends unless it has sufficient profits to pay them, either in the current year, or profits retained from previous years.

Directors' fees

These are simply payments to senior employees and are treated in the same way as other wages and salaries, as expenses in the profit and loss account. Directors may or may not also be shareholders of the company, but any payments they receive as directors are normal business expenses. If they are also shareholders, then they receive dividends as do the other shareholders.

Auditors' fees

Limited companies are required to have their accounts 'audited' – examined by a firm of independent accountants. Auditors charge fees, as you would expect, and these are also expenses in the profit and loss account.

Debentures

Limited companies can raise money by issuing debentures. As far as you are concerned, these are simply long-term loans which carry interest. The interest charges are expenses in the profit and loss account.

Corporation tax

This is a tax on companies and is included in the profit and loss account, after the calculation of net profit. It is deducted from the net profit as any other expense, but it is normally regarded as an 'appropriation' of profits as its amount varies according to the level of profits.

Reserves

Any profits which the directors decide to leave in the business rather than pay out as dividends are called *revenue reserves*. There are several different types of reserves, but this book only includes reserves which are profits left in the business.

The appropriation account

After the net profit has been calculated in the usual manner, it is followed by an *appropriation account* which shows how the profits have been distributed or retained. Any profits retained from previous years are also brought into this account.

	Corby Limited has a net profit for xxx1 of £300,000.
Example	Corporation tax on this is estimated at £60,000. The directors decide to pay out a dividend of 5p per share, of which there are 1 million. Retained profits from previous years amount to £100,000. The appropriation account of Corby would appear as follows:

Corby Limited – appropriation account for the year ended 31 December xxx1

	£
Net profit before tax	300,000
Corporation tax	60,000
Net profit for the year, after tax	240,000
Retained profits brought forward	100,000
Profits available for distribution	340,000
Dividends proposed	50,000
Retained profits carried forward	290,000

The balance sheet of a limited company

Again, many of the items which appear in the balance sheet of a sole trader, also appear in the balance sheet of a limited company. The limited company does, however, have more categories of current liability to show on its balance sheet, as it does not normally pay out its auditors' fees, corporation tax and dividends until the following year.

The other major difference is the appearance of the owners' capital section. It does not show dividends as drawings, as these have been included in the appropriation account, but it may have various reserves to include.

Using Corby Limited as an example, suppose that the 1 million shares were issued for £4.00 each. That's £1 million of 'share capital' and £3 million of 'share premium'.

The capital section at 31 December xxx1 would be as follows:

Financed by:	**£000**
Share capital	1,000
Share premium	3,000
Retained profits	290
	4,290

The current liabilities section of the balance sheet would include the unpaid corporation tax of £60,000 and the unpaid dividends of £50,000, as well as any other current liabilities.

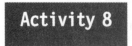

Construct the capital section of a limited company which has issued 100,000 £1 shares at £3 each, and has retained profit of £450,000.

The financial statements of other types of organization

Chapter 1 mentioned other types of organization, such as partnerships, corporations, and clubs, societies and charities. These prepare financial accounts on the same basis as sole traders and limited companies, but with some differences. Clubs, societies and charities, for example, do not exist primarily to make profit but to provide support to disadvantaged groups or services to members. For this reason, they do not call their profit and loss account by that name, but call it an *income and expenditure account*. These organizations do not have owners either, so they do not have capital. Any retained 'profits' (called 'surpluses') are called the *accumulated fund*. But in other respects, their accounts are much the same.

Regulation and control in accounting

You can see that there is a great deal of scope for preparing financial accounts which do not show a true picture. Ask yourself some questions:

- What value do we put on stocks? The cost price? The selling price?
- How should we depreciate fixed assets?
- Should we make any adjustment for the possiblity of some debtors not paying up?

The accounting profession has a range of statements and guidelines which help organizations to produce accounts which show a 'true and fair view' of the affairs of the organization. These statements and guidelines lay down procedures to be followed in cases of doubt, and limited companies are bound by law to comply with them. It is sensible if other organizations also comply with them. If they do, it means that the accounts can be relied upon to have been prepared with care and in a reasonable manner.

Summary

Now that you have completed this chapter you should understand the purpose of accounting and the difference between book-keeping, financial accounting and management accounting. You should be able to explain a variety of accounting terms, and understand the content and headings in the main financial statements. You should be able to calculate various key figures in accounting, such as the cost of goods sold, gross and net profit and working capital, and be able to prepare simple financial statements. You should appreciate the difference between 'profit' and 'cash', and have an appreciation of the form and content of the accounts of a limited company.

Review and discussion questions

1 What does accounting aim to provide?
2 What are the key differences between financial and management accounts?
3 What are the three main financial statements?
4 What does a profit and loss account show?
5 What are the main headings on a balance sheet?
6 Define the 'accounting equation'.
7 List four reasons why an organization might make a profit but have a bank overdraft.
8 Identify four items which appear only in the accounts of a limited company.

Case study

Tamara Johnson has asked for your help in compiling her profit and loss account and balance sheet for xxx1. She presents you with a list of balances from her books and records, as follows:

	£
Stock at 1 January xxx1	2,970
Debtors	3,350
Creditors	3,680
Wages and salaries	1,520
Rent and rates	1,390
Motor vehicles at cost	2,000
Purchases	5,830
Sales	10,600
Bank balance	520
Drawings	1,000
Capital at 1 January xxx1	4,300

She feels that the motor vehicle should be depreciated over five years. Stock at 31 December xxx1 is £1,780.

Prepare her trading account, profit and loss account and balance sheet for the year ending 31 December xxx1. Explain to Tamara what is meant by the phrase 'working capital', and advise her on whether she can afford to spend £3,000 on a new machine next month.

Work-based assignment

B1.1
B1.2

Write a short description of your organization's accounting systems, to include the following headings:

- the type of organization (sole trader, company, or other), and the kind of business carried on
- the method of book-keeping (manual, computerized)
- the types of revenue earned
- the main expenses incurred
- the fixed assets owned
- the current assets

You do not need to determine *values* for the above, as this information might not be available to you.

3 Managing cash resources

Learning objectives

On completion of this chapter you will be able to:

- explain the difference between cash receipts and cash payments
- describe different methods of payment
- appreciate the effect of timing of receipts and payments on cash flow
- prepare a cash budget
- consider ways of improving cash flow
- describe a simple method of recording cash transactions

Introduction

Cash is said to be the 'lifeblood' of an organization. Without cash, either already in the bank, or available to be borrowed, an organization cannot exist. Cash is needed in order to pay for the essentials from day-to-day, as well as for longer-term or less regular purchases. When we talk about 'cash', we also include money in bank accounts which is readily available. This chapter looks at different types of receipts and payments, and decribes methods of recording and controlling cash.

Receipts and payments

Receipts

Money comes in from a variety of sources. You will look at these in more detail in Chapter 4. The main sources are from the owners (capital), which usually comes in in large 'blocks' when the organization commences its activities, and from time to time when extra is needed; and from customers to whom you have sold your goods and services.

Activity 9

Where do you think the following organizations get their receipts from?

(a) a charity
(b) a medical centre
(c) a college
(d) a local authority

See Feedback section for answer to this activity.

Payments

Day-to-day payments include the following:

- to pay for materials
- to pay wages
- to purchase stationery
- to provide petrol for vehicles

Some bills are paid less frequently, say quarterly, such as

- heating and lighting bills
- insurance
- telephone
- rent and rates
- hire purchase instalments
- bank charges

Yet others are paid intermittently, such as when buying new fixed assets or repaying a loan.

It is important to ensure that cash is there when it is needed. If it is not there, then the above cannot be paid for. In some cases, this is not disastrous – if you cannot afford a new fixed asset, then maybe you can wait until you have the money. But if the wages need to be paid, then the money must be there, or your workers will refuse to work; if you do not pay your telephone bill when it is due, you might find your telephone disconnected. You can imagine the effects of such events!

Methods of payment

There are several common methods of payment for organizations to use to pay their bills, or for their customers to pay them.

RESOURCES MANAGEMENT

Cash

This was the only method of payment for a very long time – apart from the exchange of pigs and grain! People were paid their wages in cash, and used it to buy goods. Shops and manufacturers accepted cash in payment of their bills.

Cash is still widely used for small payments, and a surprising number of older people, and of course, children, have no other means of payment.

Cash has the advantage of being 'immediate' – the company concerned is paid at once, with no delay, and no risk (apart from a very small risk of forged notes). But cash is time consuming to count, check and bank. It is heavy and dirty to carry around, it attracts thieves and is easily lost. It also requires a receipt to be given, as there is no other evidence that a person has paid.

Cheques

Cheques are a more convenient method of payment than cash. A cheque is a written instruction to one person's bank, to take money out of their account and pay it into the account of another. The person paying the bill (the 'drawer' of the cheque) gives the cheque to the person supplying the goods or services (the 'payee'), and that person pays it into their bank account. The cheque then passes to the drawer's bank, who approve ('clear') it. The drawer should have sufficient money in the bank to cover the cheque at the time it is made out. If they have not, then the cheque may 'bounce', which means that the bank refuses to pay it. This is known as a 'dishonoured cheque'. The result is that the money which has been paid in to the payee's account is taken out again – which means that, in effect, they have not been paid. They then need to contact the customer to arrange some other method of payment.

When a cheque is dishonoured, the banks usually make a charge to both the parties concerned to cover their administrative costs.

Cheques are known as 'negotiable instruments' in that, in theory, they can be passed from person to person, just like cash. But payment only takes place when the cheque is passed to the drawer's bank account.

Example

A owes B £40. A gives B a cheque for the money, made out to B. Normally, B would pay this into his bank account, and it would be taken out of A's bank account. But B owes C £40. Instead of writing out a fresh cheque to C, he passes A's cheque on to C (it has to be 'endorsed', i.e. signed on the back first). C can then pass it on to D, and so on. At this stage, nothing has been taken out of A's bank account. Eventually, someone along the line pays the cheque into their bank account, and the money comes out of A's bank account.

The danger is, that A has insufficient funds, and the cheque is dishonoured. Everyone down the line is affected.

For this reason, most cheques nowadays are printed with the words 'A/C Payee' which means that they can only be paid into the account in the name of the payee – in the example above, this would be B's account. The cheque cannot be passed on in this case.

Cheque guarantee cards

Many bank customers have these cards, which guarantee that the cheque will not be dishonoured. Many cards only guarantee cheques up to the value of £50 per transaction. This means that if the customer is buying something for more than £50, the guarantee is invalid. This applies even if the customer writes out more than one cheque. For example, if the bill is £75, and the customer makes out two cheques – one for £50 and one for £25 – the guarantee does not apply.

Some guarantee cards cover the cheque up to £250.

Credit cards

These are cards issued by banks, to selected customers who are considered to be a 'good risk'.

The customer is given a 'credit limit'. The card is used to make payments to shops, etc. The amount is charged to the customer's account, who receives a monthly bill from the credit card company. The customer can choose to pay off the bill in full, with no interest charges if payment is made within a specified time, or to spread payment over several months, with interest. For the supplier, the amount can be paid into the bank as with a cheque, and the money is paid into the account at once. But the supplier does have to pay a charge for each transaction.

Examples include Access, Visa, Mastercard.

Debit cards

These are cards which transfer funds immediately from the customer's account to the supplier's account. They are extremely safe from the supplier's point of view. For the customer, it means that the money is taken out of their account immediately. This makes them less attractive to the customer than the credit card. There are no interest charges as the money is taken out of the customer's account at once.

An example is SWITCH.

Both credit cards and debit cards can be used at Electronic Point-of-Sale (EPOS) terminals, and the funds are then transferred directly betweeen accounts. This is known as Electronic Funds Transfer (EFT).

Store cards

These work like credit cards, in that the customer receives a monthly bill, and the store obtains payment monthly, from the finance company with whom they have the account.

Charge cards

These are issued by finance companies such as American Express and Diners Club. They are issued only to people who meet certain criteria with regard to income. The company who accepts these cards has virtually no risk at all, but the customer has to pay off the monthly bill in full each month.

Standing orders and direct debits

These payments are made automatically by the bank on a regular basis, say once a month. The funds are taken out of the payer's accounts and transferred to the payee's account. The advantage to the customer is that they do not have to remember to make the payment, and do not have the trouble of making out a cheque or posting it.

The difference between the two methods is that with a standing order it is the bank of the payer which initiates the transfer, with a direct debit it is the bank of the payee. Some people feel that they have less control over direct debits, because they usually give the payee the right to change the amount from time to time, but direct debits are only used by reputable organizations and they can be cancelled by the payer if necessary.

BACS transfers

These are also transfers made between banks, whereby the payer notifies the bank each time the payment is to be made. They are commonly used by organizations to pay their employees' wages. The bank is given a list of employees, their bank details, and the net wage, and makes a single payment out of the payer's account and individual payments into the employees' accounts.

CHAPS payments

These are used where funds need to be transferred between banks very quickly. They are used a great deal by solicitors in the buying and selling of houses. Monies need to be moved from the buyer to the seller, and from the seller to the person *he* is buying from, and so on, all at the same time. They are often initiated by telephone, followed by written confirmation.

This type of bank transfer has different versions according to whether the funds are to be transferred within the country or between other countries, and the level of computerization within the banks concerned. Nowadays, many customers are linked to their banks by computer, making these payments even more automated.

Activity 10

Which method of payment do you think is likely to be most suitable in the following situations:

(a) payment of monthly rental for machinery
(b) payment of £1.50 for postage stamps
(c) payment for goods from a mail-order catalogue
(d) payment for theatre tickets ordered over the telephone
(e) payment of wages to 500 employees each month

See Feedback section for answer to this activity.

Investigate 5

Investigate the methods of payment used by your organization, both for receiving money and for paying money out. Are there any suggestions you can make to improve the speed at which monies are received?

Timing of cash receipts and payments

Cash does not always come in and go out on a regular basis. The timing of receipts and payments is crucial to survival. Most organizations operate on a 'credit' basis. This means that they buy and sell goods and services, but the money does not change hands immediately. It may change hands in the next month or two, or be spread over a longer period.

Do you remember the name given to people who owe money to an organization? They are called debtors. And people to whom the organization owes money are called creditors.

Some businesses do not allow credit at all. Retailers are a good example. Shoppers have to pay immediately, even if by credit card, before they are allowed to remove the goods.

You can see from Section 2 of this chapter that there are many different methods of payment which might speed up or slow down the process of making and receiving payment.

Preparing a cash budget

A cash budget is normally prepared on a monthly basis over six or twelve months. Some organizations might produce it on a weekly basis. The main purpose is to ensure that the organization has sufficient cash when it needs it. If the cash budget shows that there will be insufficient cash at any time, then action can be taken to avoid the situation, or to negotiate extra funds, perhaps with an overdraft.

Example

Jenny is starting a printing business. She has the opportunity to buy some premises for £30,000, and she will need a printing machine costing £24,000. Her own car is not suitable for transporting either the raw materials or the finished goods to her customers, so she is buying a van for £8,000. Her grandmother has left her £70,000 in her will, which Jenny has already put into a business bank account. The premises, machine and van are all to be paid for on 1 January xxx1, when she starts her business.

In January, she expects to be stocking up with paper, inks, etc. and advertising her services to local businesses and the public. She does not expect to get any orders until February. She expects twenty-five per cent of her customers to pay at once, and she is giving two months' credit to local businesses. Her suppliers have insisted that she pays immediately for the first two months' supplies, but after that they will give her one month's credit. She is employing an assistant from February, who will be paid £500 a month, on the 28th of each month. She needs £700 a month for herself to live on. Initial advertising in January will cost £2,000, payable at once, but after that she is taking a regular space in the local newspaper costing £200 a month, payable one month in arrears.

Her sales and purchases are expected to be as follows:

	Jan £	Feb £	March £	April £	May £	June £
Sales	nil	4,000	6,000	8,000	10,000	12,000
Purchases	5,000	5,000	6,000	7,000	8,000	9,000

In order to prepare the cash budget, she needs to set out exactly when money will be coming in and out. The sales do not commence until February, so there is no money coming in in January. For each month's sales, only twenty-five per cent will pay at once. The remainder will come in two months later – so, in February she will receive £1,000 (twenty-five per cent of £4,000 sold), and the other £3,000 will come in in April. It is a good idea to set this out in a table:

	Jan £	Feb £	March £	April £	May £	June £
Sales	nil	4,000	6,000	8,000	10,000	12,000
Paid at once (25%)		1,000	1,500	2,000	2,500	3,000
Paid in 2 months		3,000	4,500	6,000	7,500	9,000
i.e.		April	May	June	July	August

The same can be done for her purchases:

	Jan £	Feb £	March £	April £	May £	June £
Purchases	5,000	5,000	6,000	7,000	8,000	9,000
Paid at once	5,000	5,000				
Paid in 1 month			6,000	7,000	8,000	9,000
i.e.			April	May	June	July

Her monthly advertising of £200 is also paid one month after the advert is placed.

Her cash budget for the first six months of trading is as follows:

	Jan £	Feb £	March £	April £	May £	June £	Total £
Receipts							
Sales – cash		1,000	1,500	2,000	2,500	3,000	10,000
Sales – credit				3,000	4,500	6,000	13,500
Total receipts		1,000	1,500	5,000	7,000	9,000	23,500
Payments							
Premises	30,000						30,000
Machinery	24,000						24,000
Van	8,000						8,000
Purchases	5,000	5,000		6,000	7,000	8,000	31,000
Wages	500	500	500	500	500	500	3,000
Drawings	700	700	700	700	700	700	4,200
Advertising	2,000		200	200	200	500	3,100
Total payments	70,200	6,200	1,400	7,400	8,400	9,700	103,300
Opening balance	70,000	–200	–5,400	–5,300	–7,700	–9,100	70,000
Total receipts	0	1,000	1,500	5,000	7,000	9,000	23,500
	70,000	800	–3,900	–300	–700	–100	93,500
Total payments	70,200	6,200	1,400	7,400	8,400	9,700	103,300
Closing balance	–200	–5,400	–5,300	–7,700	–9,100	–9,800	–9,800

You can see that after the first month, Jenny is not going to have enough money in the bank. This is quite common for new businesses. The situation will gradually improve over the next six months, as she will then start to have more coming in than she is paying out. In July, for example, she will get in £7,500 owing from her May customers, plus say £3,000 from her July cash customers, and she will only be paying out £9,000 for supplies, plus her £1,400 regular payments.

However, she needs to be aware that this is going to happen, and think what to do about it.

Managing shortfalls

Jenny is going to have a shortfall of cash for several months. There are several things she could do about it.

Apply for an overdraft

The bank might be sympathetic to a request for an overdraft for this period. The amount she requires is relatively small, and she does have premises which could be sold to pay off the overdraft if her business fails. The bank will want to look at her cash budget and to see if she is making a profit. We cannot tell whether she is from the figures we are given, but it would seem that she is selling her goods for more than she is purchasing, although we don't know how much of her materials she is keeping in stock. If she is profitable, then an overdraft is possible.

Find other methods of financing fixed assets

She is paying out a lot for her premises, machinery and van. In the next chapter you will look at sources of finance for businesses in more detail, but Jenny could consider paying for these assets over a period of time, rather than all at once. She could perhaps take out a mortgage for the premises, for, say, half the cost, and pay over ten years. She could consider buying the van on hire purchase over two years. This would improve her cash flow considerably.

Review the credit given to customers

Jenny allows her business customers two months to pay. Perhaps this could be reduced to one month. She could offer incentives to them to pay promptly such as giving them a discount of two per cent if they pay within thirty days.

Reducing the credit in this way could completely wipe out the need for an overdraft at all.

Take advantage of credit given by suppliers

This can be a source of 'free' credit, unless suppliers charge a penalty for late payment. Delaying payments to creditors means that the cash is retained in the business bank account for longer, or the overdraft is reduced.

It is important, though, not to antagonize creditors such that they refuse to supply.

Managing excesses

Eventually, Jenny might find she has more cash in the bank than she needs. As most business current accounts do not pay interest, she needs to find something to do with the money which will bring in some income.

The choice depends on her future plans. If she is likely to need the money in the near future, then she will want to invest it where she can withdraw it when required. A bank deposit account or building society would be a good idea for her.

Jenny is only a small business owner. Larger businesses, with more cash, have a wider choice of deposits, sometimes overnight deposits. Although they might be investing for only a short time, the interest on a large amount of money is substantial.

If she is not likely to need the money in the near future, then there are longer term investments she could consider. As a sole trader, she could withdraw the money and invest it in a variety of personal investments. This subject is not covered at this stage in your studies. A large company could invest in the shares of other companies.

If this business is profitable, she might want to expand. After all, her own business should be making more money for her investment than she could get elsewhere, otherwise there is no financial reason to be running her own business! But remember, in large organizations and limited companies, there are other rewards for shareholders than just making profit.

Activity 11

Prepare a cash budget for the first six months, for the following business, which intends to commence on 1 January xxx1:

Initial capital invested in
the bank   £23,000
Fixed assets to be acquired
on 1 January   Plant and machinery £10,000
                  Motor vehicles   £12,000
Sales   £2,000 in January and February
        £4,000 in March and April
        £6,000 in May and June

Ten per cent are for immediate payment, the remainder paying one month later.

Purchases equal seventy per cent of sales. They are to be paid for at once in the first three months, with one month's credit thereafter.

Premises rental is £1,000 a quarter, payable on the first on January, April, July and October.

Postage of five per cent of the selling price is payable one month after sale. Wages of £700 a month are paid at the end of each month.

Discuss ways in which the cash shortages and/or excesses could be managed.

See Feedback section for answer to this activity.

Using the cash budget

As well as being used to highlight shortages and excesses of cash, the cash budget should also be used to check actual receipts and payments, to ensure that they are in line with the budget. Differences between budget and actual should be investigated, and if necessary the budget for future periods should be amended.

An out-of-date budget is of no use at all.

Record keeping for receipts and payments

These days, most organizations handle actual cash as little as possible. Bank accounts and electronic methods of transferring funds are more common. Most cash received is paid into the bank at once, and payments are rarely made in cash.

Unless you are involved in the book-keeping of your organization, it is unlikely that you will be handling cash and bank transactions yourself. However, it is useful to look at some of the ways of recording and controlling these transactions.

Keeping a record of bank transactions

This is often called a 'cash book' – even though it does not refer to cash itself! Layouts vary widely, depending on the needs of the organization. Some organizations keep separate books for receipts and payments, with columns to analyse the transactions.

Recording monies paid into the bank

An example of the record of monies paid in might be as follows:

Date	Details	Pay-in slip no.	Amount banked	Cash sales	From debtors	Rent rec'd	Other receipts
xxx1			£	£	£	£	£
Jan 1	Sales of goods			1,000			
	Debtors				2,000		
	Rent					100	
	Sale of van						5,000
		001	8,100				
Jan 2	Sales of goods			1,500			
	Debtors				6,000		
		002	7,500				
Jan 3	Debtors	BGC	4,000		4,000		
	Debtors	CH	8,000		8,000		

Note – the reference 'BGC' means 'Bank Giro Credit', indicating that the money has been paid in directly by the customer. The reference 'CH' indicates a CHAPS payment.

Recording monies paid out of the bank

An example might be as follows:

Date	Details	Cq	Total	Creditors	Wages	Motor	Rent	Other
xxx1			£	£	£	£	£	£
Jan 1	P. Bloggs	123	2,500	2,500				
	J. Smith	124	1,500	1,500				
	L. Taylor	125	2,200	2,200				
Jan 2	Wages	BACS	1,800		1,800			
	ABC Property	DD	800				800	
Jan 3	Furniture	126						3,400
	Petrol	127				40		

Keeping track of the balance at the bank

The balance at the bank should be ascertained regularly – in some organizations, this is done daily, or even after every transaction. At the very least, it should be done weekly, by taking the balance at the beginning of the week, adding the monies paid in, and deducting the monies paid out, as the above records illustrate. Do not rely on the bank to notify you of the balance in your account, as this will usually not be up to date. Recent receipts and payments might not yet have got through to the bank – your own internal record should be more reliable.

Checking the accuracy of bank records

It is important that the accuracy of your bank records is checked, otherwise mistakes will not be discovered or corrected, and incorrect decisions could be made. The bank also keeps a record of an organization's transactions, and will send a statement as required. This should be checked against the internal records of bank transactions, and any queries investigated. This is known as performing a 'bank reconciliation'.

Summary

Now that you have completed this chapter you will appreciate the difference between cash receipts and cash payments, and will be able to describe different methods of payment and how they are used. You will be able to prepare a cash budget showing receipts, payments and the closing balance and be able to identify shortfalls and excesses. You will also be able to explain ways in which cash flow can be improved, and be aware of a method of recording cash transactions so as to keep track of cash movements on a regular basis.

Review and discussion questions

1 Why is cash control important?
2 Identify and describe six methods of payment
3 What are the three sections on a cash budget?
4 What action can be taken to avoid a cash shortfall?
5 Is an excess of cash a good thing?
6 How can you check that your bank balance is correct?

Case study

Leslie started his business twelve months ago, with money from a redundancy pay-out, and a loan of £10,000 from his father. His business is profitable, and he has stayed in credit at the bank, finishing his first year with a balance of £12,000. His sales are expected to be £20,000 a month over the next year, with materials costing £15,000 a month. He gives his customers a month's credit, but lately they have been taking longer than this to pay. He does not want to lose them, and he wonders if he should extend credit to two months, in the hope of attracting extra customers. He pays for his supplies as he buys them, because he doesn't like to owe people money. Customers from last year still owe him £25,000 on 1 January. Annual rates and insurance are due on 1 April, totalling £5,000, and he would like to buy a new machine as soon as possible. His father is happy to let him repay the loan when he can, but he would like to pay it back soon as he does not pay any interest on it. During his first year of trading, he has managed without any drawings, but his wife is leaving work next month to have a baby, and he needs to know how much he can withdraw to support his family.

Advise Leslie as to his cash position over the next few months, making any assumptions you feel are necessary. Respond to his suggestion that he should allow customers two months' credit and suggest any alternatives to his current situation which might help.

Work-based assignment

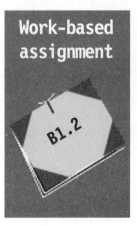

B1.2

Identify an area at work where cash budgets are prepared. Obtain a copy of the budget and explanations to back up its preparation and use. Critically evaluate the preparation and use of the budget, identify any areas of weakness, and make suggestions for improvement.

4 Sources of finance

Learning objectives

On completion of this chapter you will be able to:

- explain the stages in an organization's life when finance might be required
- identify a range of different sources of finance
- describe the suitability of different sources in different circumstances
- consider *internal* sources of finance as well as external
- understand the need to match the source of finance with its purpose
- appreciate the need for negotiation in cash budget allocations

Introduction

Finance is needed at various stages in an organization's life, and for different purposes.

The three main stages are shown in Figure 4.1.

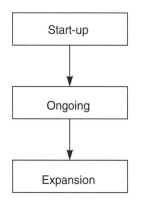

Figure 4.1
Three main stages in
an organization's life

There are many different sources of finance available to organizations. Choosing the correct source can be difficult, and depends on a number of factors such as:

- *why* finance is required
- *how long* it is likely to be needed
- *how much* is needed

This chapter examines some of the occasions on which finance is required, and the alternatives available.

Reasons for requiring finance

Start-up finance

When a business first commences, it will need certain things in order to get going. It may even need to conduct market or product research before it can start trading at all.

Some of the things for which finance will be needed on start-up are as follows:

- fixed assets
- initial stocks of materials
- test production runs
- recruitment and selection of staff
- training of staff
- market research
- advertising
- deposits on rented property
- costs of setting up control systems

Start-up finance is often the most difficult to obtain. The organization has no track record of success to attract investors or lenders. It has no existing resources to fall back on.

Ongoing finance

This is needed to keep the business running on a day-to-day basis. Finance is needed for things such as:

- replacing stocks of materials
- further production runs
- staff wages and salaries
- tax and VAT bills
- paying creditors
- insurance
- heat and light
- general advertising
- purchasing and selling
- delivery costs

Ongoing finance might be easier to obtain. The organization will have built up some of its own resources, and it will have a track record of past successes. It will have a customer base, and staff loyalty, with systems and procedures for control in place.

Expansion finance

Some of the items needed on expansion are as for start-up, e.g. fixed assets and training. Much depends on the type of expansion programme. Types of expansion include:

- replacement of old equipment and methods with new
- expansion of existing premises
- relocation to bigger premises
- merger with another company
- take over of another company

Finance may also be needed to pay redundancy costs if necessary.

The availability of expansion finance will depend heavily on the organization's past performance and previous history of managing its financial resources.

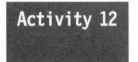

Suggest ten possible reasons why a supermarket might require finance.

See Feedback section for answer to this activity.

Identify six reasons why your own organization has required finance in the last twelve months.

Sources of finance

There are many different sources of finance to suit different purposes. These are discussed now.

Owners

In a sole trader's business, this means from the sole trader and his or her family and friends. This source could be limited. Many sole traders commence with almost nothing but their skill. Finance comes from savings, redundancy monies, winnings and inheritances.

In a partnership, there are more people to contribute to the finance required, but they still have the same limitations as a sole trader.

In a limited company, the owners are the shareholders. There are often more of them – hundreds of thousands in some public limited companies – and they have the added bonus of limited liability for the company's debts. So they are often more willing to risk the investment.

Raising capital by the issue of shares in a public limited company is expensive. It entails the production of various financial statements and declarations, and must comply with strict and complex legislation.

Shareholders, indeed all owners, want a return on their investment, i.e. a share of the profits. In a limited company, this means that there will be an expectation that some of the profits will be paid out to the shareholders in the form of dividends.

Raising capital from the owners, whoever they are, is usually only done on start-up or when expansion is planned. It is suitable for long-term finance.

Banks

Banks are a very common source of finance for all types of organization, whether in the long term or short term. There are different types of bank, including merchant banks who are specifically involved in providing finance to large companies, and the commercial high street banks.

Overdrafts

An overdraft is generally intended to finance short-term needs, although it is true that many organizations have an almost permanent overdraft. An overdraft 'facility' should be negotiated in advance with the bank. An agreed limit is set, and the business is allowed to overdraw by up to this amount at any one time. Interest charges are fairly high, but they are only charged on the actual level of the overdraft in existence, even though a higher limit might have been agreed. So, if a business negotiates a limit of £10,000, but is only overdrawn by £5,000, interest is only payable on the £5,000.

An overdraft can, in theory, be 'called in' for repayment at any time.

Bank loans

These are generally cheaper than overdrafts, and are usually for specific purposes such as the purchase of fixed assets. There are many different types of loan, some with fixed interest rates, some with variable rates. Some charge interest on the whole loan, and the repayments are a set amount each month. Some charge interest only on the outstanding amount.

Some loans require an amount to be repaid each month, others are repaid at the end of the period of the loan. There is often an insurance policy attached to this type of loan, which matures (is paid out) when the loan needs repaying. Most banks also insist that lenders pay an insurance premium to cover them against non-payment due to ill-health, etc.

Bank loans are usually for short/medium finance, say five years. The lender may ask the borrower for some form of security, i.e. something the borrower has which can be sold if the debt is not repaid.

A bank loan is unlikely to be granted if the owners do not already have a similar amount or more invested in the business.

Mortgages

These are long-term loans used for the purchase of buildings. Banks and building societies offer mortgages. As with bank loans, there are many different schemes for the payment of interest and the capital itself. A mortgage is always 'secured' on the asset it has been used to purchase, so that the lender is entitled to that asset if the borrower defaults.

Activity 13

Obtain details of overdraft, loan and mortgage facilities for businesses, from TWO banks. Make a comparison of the interest rates and methods of payment, and any security they require. You will probably find different terms are available for different sizes and durations of loan.

Finance companies

These give finance for the purchase of specific assets, such as machinery, motor vehicles and office equipment. Hire purchase is a common type of finance from these companies.

With hire purchase, the buyer does not own the assets until the final payment has been made. If he defaults during the term of the agreement (typically two to five years), there are strict rules as to whether or not the finance company can claim back the asset.

The interest rate is usually fixed at the outset of the agreement.

Some finance companies give 'interest-free' credit for payment in a short period of time, say one year. In many cases this is not strictly interest free. The purchase price may have been inflated to take account of the lost interest; the buyer may be obliged to take out insurance on the item; or he may be expected to take out 'Payment Protection Insurance' (PPI) to cover the repayments if he falls ill. Requests for such finance are often refused if the buyer does not make one of these additional 'voluntary' payments.

It pays to shop around for these deals, to find the best.

Leasing

Leasing is suitable for a variety of assets. Leases can be long term (for items such as buildings) to short term (for items such as equiment and vehicles).

The item is never owned by the lessee, but remains the property of the lessor. The advantage to the lessee is that the lease can be terminated when the item is to be replaced, and a newer, more up-to-date model leased instead. It is ideal for items which involve technological change.

Some lease agreements do allow the lessee to purchase the item for a small fee at the end of the term.

Debentures

These are used by public limited companies to raise long-term funds for major activities. They are similar to shares, in that they are issued to a large number of lenders rather than just one, and they can be bought and sold by other debenture holders.

As far as you are concerned, debentures are simply ways of raising long-term finance. The loans carry annual interest at a fixed rate, which has to be paid without fail, and are often secured on the company's assets. The debentures fall due for repayment at a fixed time in the future.

Government assistance

There are several types of government assistance for businesses. Some of these are:

• regional grants and subsidies in certain areas, to certain types of business
• tax incentives for shareholders to invest in companies
• tax reliefs on certain types of expenditure
• local authority grants
• the Loan Guarantee Scheme, which guarantees the repayment of up to ninety per cent of a business loan from a bank

Voluntary finance providers

A number of organizations provide finance for particular purposes. The Prince's Youth Trust is an example, which provides finance to the young unemployed to set up their own businesses.

TV companies and newspaper groups also provide support through competitions.

Business angels

These are individuals who invest in young companies which they see as having potential. Often the product or service is something unusual which catches the attention of the investor. It is often a more 'risky' idea, which banks will not get involved in. The business angel is attracted by tax reliefs.

Activity 14

Which source of finance would you consider most suitable for each of the following requirements, and why?

(a) the acquisition of a delivery van
(b) the acquisition of new premises
(c) the purchase of materials over the next twelve months
(d) moving premises to a deprived area
(e) the development of a new, revolutionary product

You might have more than one source for each, which is fine.

See Feedback section for answer to this activity.

RESOURCES MANAGEMENT

Internal sources of finance

This is perhaps the first place that organizations should look to when they require finance. If the organization has built up profits which have not been distributed, there may be funds available within the business.

If the company is part of a group, there may be funds available within the group.

Internal funds are not really 'free'. If they are currently invested in other areas, then there will be lost interest if the funds are withdrawn. Even if they are not already invested, they could be used for other purposes, and therefore the profits from that other purpose will be lost. All capital costs money, including that raised internally.

Working capital

Working capital is the finance required for day-to-day activities. Money is needed to buy stocks, to support debtors who do not pay immediately, and to provide cash for regular expenses such as wages, heat and light, etc. The overdraft is commonly used for such items, and is a sensible means of borrowing for this type of finance.

Managing working capital needs is often more important than managing long-term finance, as decisions have to be made very quickly, and funds have to be available at once.

Organizations should make use of the credit facilities offered by suppliers, to pay in one or two months. This is a source of 'free' credit, unless the suppliers impose penalties for late payment.

Working capital should always be financed by short-term methods.

Matching the type of finance with its purpose

The type of finance obtained should be suitable for the purpose for which it is required. A long-term project requires long-term finance, while a short-term project should be financed on a short-term basis.

As an example of how *not* to finance expenditure, many householders re-mortgage their homes to provide extra funds to purchase a car. The mortgage is repaid over twenty-five years or so, but the car needs replacing after three or four years. They are still repaying the mortgage, including the cost of the car, twenty-one years after having disposed of it! And how do they finance the next car?

Negotiating cash budget allocations

If you are responsible for a budget, it must be negotiated carefully to ensure that you are able to meet your objectives within the budget allocated to you.

First, identify any major budget requirements such as for fixed assets or one-off items. If these affect the operation of your section, then it is important to ascertain the likelihood of obtaining them. This will affect your general budget requirements.

Then, identify the month-by-month needs of your section, and produce a plan of expenditure. This may be based on previous years' experiences, taking into account changes for the coming year.

If your budget request is refused, or needs to be modified, be prepared to identify the effects of the modification, to support your case.

Summary

Now that you have completed this chapter, you should be able to identify a number of occasions when organizations require finance, and you should be able to consider sources of finance appropriate to each occasion. You should understand the different sources of finance available, and their characteristics.

Review and discussion questions

1 What are the three stages when finance might be required by an organization?
2 Identify and describe four methods of long-term finance (five years or longer)
3 Identify and describe three methods of short-term finance (three years or shorter)
4 Why is it important to match the source of finance with its purpose?

Case study

Town and Country Furnishings is owned by Heather and Paul. They are thinking of expanding, by moving to bigger premises in a different area. They make and sell middle-quality furniture and furnishings, buying most of their materials from wholesalers. Although the business is profitable, it does not have much cash. Paul is also keen to extend the business by importing Chinese antiques, for which he feels there is a market, but Heather feels this is too risky a venture.

The expansion will require extra stocks of materials, and additional staff to manufacture the furniture. It could be some months before this is sold, as the firm has not yet got orders for more than their current production. The present delivery vehicles are in need of replacement.

Write a report to Heather and Paul outlining some possible sources of finance which could be considered.

Work-based assignment

B1.1
B1.2

Identify three possible requirements for finance in your organization, preferably in your own section or area of control. Include one each of short-, medium- and long-term (e.g. for a special project). Considering the nature of your organization, suggest appropriate methods of financing each requirement, giving details of costs, methods of repayment and the advantages and disadvantages of the methods you have considered.

5 Analysing financial statements

Learning objectives

By the end of this chapter you will be able to:

- understand why analysis of financial statements is important
- identify different types of ratio for different situations
- calculate a range of ratios
- interpret the ratios and draw conclusions where appropriate

Introduction

The chapter explains the techniques involved in analysing financial statements to determine how well, or otherwise, the organization is doing. Very few people are capable of reading a set of accounts for an organization, and determining with any degree of accuracy whether that organization is successful or not – and why.

There are many different ways of analysing the financial statements, and this chapter only considers the most common methods of analysis. It describes a range of calculations which can be performed on the financial accounts, but, more importantly what these calculations show – or do not show, as the case may be.

There is no foolproof way of analysing accounts. You will probably find that a firm is doing well in one area, but not so well in another, and often clear conclusions are impossible to draw.

Why analysis is important

Take the following example of four companies:

	Turnover (£m)	Profit (£m)
Company A	10,000	1,200
Company B	12,500	1,400
Company C	8,250	1,000
Company D	18,400	1,900

Which is the best company?

Well, it all depends on the criteria you employ. The 'best' in terms of turnover and profit is Company D. The worst is Company C.

But how do they fare if you compare the amount of profit with the turnover? You would expect Company D, with its large turnover, to have a large profit. Is it as large as it should be? You would expect Company C with its small turnover to have a small profit. Is it as small as you would expect?

In order to improve on your first reaction, you need to compare the profit of each company with its turnover. A common way of doing this is to calculate the profit as a percentage of turnover, i.e.

$$\frac{\text{Profit}}{\text{Turnover}} \times 100$$

The calculations are as follows:

Company A $\quad \dfrac{1,200}{10,000} \times 100 = 12\%$

Company B $\quad \dfrac{1,400}{12,500} \times 100 = 11.2\%$

Company C $\quad \dfrac{1,000}{8,250} \times 100 = 12.1\%$

Company D $\quad \dfrac{1,900}{18,400} \times 100 = 10.3\%$

These percentages show that Company C actually produces more profit per £ of turnover than any of the other three companies – and Company D produces the least.

Whether this is important or not depends on the company's objectives, and those of the person analysing the results. But this exercise does show you that simply taking figures at their face value does not necessarily give full information.

What is ratio analysis?

Ratio analysis is a collection of calculations which are performed on an organization's financial results in order to provide additional support for decision making. A ratio is a comparison of one figure with another. In the previous section, this was a comparison of profit with turnover. Ratios are also sometimes referred to as 'performance indicators'.

Ratios are often expressed in percentage terms, but this is not the only method of expression, as you will see later in this chapter.

Some alternative means of expression are:

- As a value per unit, e.g. if sales were £40,000 and there were 20 employees, this could be expressed as £2,000 per employee.
- As a fraction, e.g. if total costs were £50,000 and salaries amounted to £25,000, you could say that salaries were half of total costs.
- As a straight comparison, e.g. if the cost of advertising was £10,000 and the resulting sales were £100,000, you could say that sales compared to advertising costs were 10:1 (i.e. every £1 spent on advertising resulted in £10 of sales).

Once a ratio has been calculated, it should be compared with the same ratio for previous periods, other organizations, industry standards, and your own expectations.

Types of ratio

In theory, you can compare any figure with any other figure, providing that the result has some meaning to the user. However, there are five main types of ratio, as follows:

1 peformance ratios – to measure profitability
2 solvency ratios – to measure liquidity (i.e. how much cash or 'near cash' the organization has)
3 efficiency ratios – to measure how well assets are used to create revenue and profit
4 gearing ratios – to measure the capital structure and financing
5 security ratios – to measure the value of investors' funds

Information from which ratios are calculated

A great deal of information is available from the financial statements of an organization, supplemented by additional figures from the management accounts.

Throughout this chapter, the following financial statements will be used to calculate appropriate ratios to analyse the financial performance of an organization:

AJM Limited
Trading and profit and loss account
for the year ended 31 December xxx1

	£	£
Sales		100,000
Less cost of sales:		
Opening stock	13,000	
Purchases	62,000	
	75,000	
Less closing stock	15,000	
		60,000
Gross profit		40,000
Less expenses		30,000
Net profit before tax		10,000
Taxation		2,000
Net profit after tax		8,000
Dividends		1,000
Retained profit for the year		7,000

Balance sheet at 31 December xxx1

	£	£
Fixed assets		77,000
Current assets		
Stocks	15,000	
Debtors	12,000	
Bank and cash	8,000	
	35,000	
Less Current liabilities		
Creditors	22,000	
Working capital		13,000
		90,000
Less Long-term liabilities		10,000
		80,000
Financed by:		
Ordinary shares of £1 each		73,000
Profit and loss account		7,000
		80,000

Performance ratios

These measure the level of profitability of the business.

Gross profit percentage or gross margin

This measures the gross profit as a percentage of the sales revenue. It shows how much of the selling price of goods results in gross profit.

$$\text{Gross profit percentage} = \frac{\text{Gross profit}}{\text{Sales}} \times 100$$

For AJM the gross profit percentage is:

$$\frac{40,000}{100,000} \times 100 = 40\%$$

This shows that for every £1 of goods sold, 40p gross profit was made.

If last year's percentage was, say only thirty per cent, this could be because of a higher cost of goods sold, or lower selling prices. Both of these would result in lower gross profit. There is no 'standard' percentage which organizations achieve – whether the percentage is good or bad depends on the type and size of organization. But obviously, a higher percentage is better than a lower one.

Gross profit mark-up percentage

This shows similar information to the margin percentage, except that *cost* of sales is used to compare to the gross profit. It is often used to work out a selling price, if the cost is known.

$$\text{Gross profit mark-up percentage} = \frac{\text{Gross profit}}{\text{Cost of sales}} \times 100$$

For AJM, the gross profit mark-up percentage is:

$$\frac{40,000}{60,000} \times 100 = 66\tfrac{2}{3}\%$$

This shows that for every £1 which goods cost, 66⅔p has been added to reach the selling price. As with the gross margin percentage, it should be compared with last year's, and a higher percentage is better than a lower one.

Net profit percentage

This shows how much *net* profit has been made as a percentage of sales. It is the figure most often used to compare with other companies, and is often published in the financial newspapers if it is a public company. The figure of profit is usually the net profit *before* tax, as the amount of tax is not always related only to the level of profit.

$$\text{Net profit percentage} = \frac{\text{Net profit}}{\text{Sales}} \times 100$$

For AJM, the net profit percentage is:

$$\frac{10,000}{100,000} \times 100 = 10\%$$

This shows that for every £1 of sales, 10p of net profit has resulted. Again, a higher percentage is better than a lower one.

Return on capital employed (ROCE)

This compares the net profit with the amount of money (capital) invested in the business. It shows the *return* which the investors can say their money has earned.

There are several different meanings of the phrase 'capital employed'. The ordinary shareholders are usually the main investors, so their money (including any reserves) is part of the capital employed. It is also possible to say that the preference shareholders funds should be included too, and maybe even the long-term loans.

There is no particular 'best' way of performing the calculation. For our purposes we will take capital employed to mean all shareholders funds.

$$\text{ROCE} = \frac{\text{Net profit before tax}}{\text{Total shareholders' funds}} \times 100$$

For AJM, the return on capital employed is:

$$\frac{10,000}{80,000} \times 100 = 12.5\%$$

This shows that for every £1 invested, a return of 12.5p has been made. Out of this, the taxation must be paid, and the remainder belongs to the shareholders.

Activity 15

From the following data, calculate the four profitability ratios:

	£
Sales	50,000
Cost of sales	30,000
Gross profit	20,000
Expenses	15,000
Net profit before tax	5,000
Capital employed	100,000

See Feedback section for answer to this activity.

Solvency ratios

These measure the ability of the company to pay its debts when they fall due. A company is 'solvent' if it has sufficient cash, or assets which can quickly be turned into cash, compared with the debts which will need paying. Cash and near-cash assets are called 'liquid' assets.

Obviously, cash and bank balances are highly liquid, but it is common to regard debtors as being liquid too – if they are likely to pay up in time to help pay the creditors. It is also possible to include stocks as liquid assets.

There are two main liquidity ratios – one including stocks, and one not.

The current ratio

This compares current assets with current liabilities.

The current ratio = current assets:current liabilities

For AJM, the current ratio is:

35,000:22,000 = 1.6:1

RESOURCES MANAGEMENT

To get the answer, you divide the current assets (35), by the current liabilities (22). The ratio shows that for every £1 of current liabilities, there is £1.60 in cash or near cash with which to pay the liabilities. If last year's ratio was 1.8:1, there could have been higher current assets, or lower current liabilities.

The 'standard' for the current ratio is generally 2:1, i.e. £2 of current assets for every £1 of current liabilities, but many organizations manage on less than this and still feel comfortable that they can pay their current liabilities. Some industries whose customers pay mostly in cash (such as supermarkets), have very low ratios as they have access to large amounts of cash very quickly, and have few debtors.

The ratio should be compared to previous periods, to detect any possible 'slowing down', which could result in a cash shortage. Creditors are interested in this ratio, as it indicates how likely the firm is to be able to pay them.

You might think it would be a good idea to have a high current ratio, say 4:1. This is not normally good practice. Money which is sitting in current assets does not earn anything for the business. Stocks on shelves mean that money is tied up doing nothing; outstanding debtors are borrowing your money for free; cash and bank balances often earn no interest. So unless excess stock is needed for a large order, or cash is needed to purchase fixed assets, current assets should be kept to a reasonable level.

The acid test ratio (quick ratio)

This measures liquidity *excluding* the stock, where it is felt that stock is not easily turned into cash. This is true where the stock is of raw materials which need to be converted into saleable goods, or finished goods which take some time to sell. Even if they sell fairly quickly, it might be some time before the debtors pay up.

The acid test ratio = current assets minus stock:current liabilities

For AJM, the acid test ratio is:

35,000 − 15,000:22,000, or 20,000:22,000 = 0.91:1

This means that for every £1 of current liabilities, there is only 91p in liquid funds with which to pay them. The usual standard for this ratio is 1:1, but if it falls too low then creditors will be concerned, and may refuse to supply the company. 0.9:1 is probably acceptable, though, if you consider that not all creditors will need paying immediately – and in AJM's case, £3,000 of the creditors figure includes taxation and dividends, which will not need to be paid for some months.

Activity 16

Calculate two liquidity ratios from the following data, and comment on your results:

	£
Stocks	35,000
Debtors	20,000
Bank balance	5,000
Creditors	40,000

See Feedback section for answer to this activity.

Efficiency ratios

These cover the use of assets, either fixed or current, or both. Those which involve current assets measure the *speed* with which current assets are converted into cash, so they are closely linked to the solvency ratios above. Those which involve fixed assets measure the amount of revenue or profit compared to the fixed assets used to earn it.

Stock turnover

This measures how quickly the business sells its stock – how many times the stock 'turns over' in a year.

$$\text{Rate of stock turnover} = \frac{\text{Cost of sales}}{\text{Average stock held throughout the year}}$$

$$\text{Average stock held} = \frac{\text{Opening stock + Closing stock}}{2}$$

For AJM, the average stock held is:

$$\frac{13,000 + 15,000}{2} = 14,000$$

and the rate of stock turnover is:

$$\frac{60,000}{14,000} = 4.3 \text{ times}$$

This shows that stock turns over 4.3 times throughout the year. You might understand this idea better if you think of it like this:

Date	Stock bought	Stock sold	Stock on hand	Cost of goods sold
January 1	£13,000 $\xrightarrow{\ +\ }$		£13,000	
March 20		£13,000 $\xrightarrow{\ =\ }$	NIL	£13,000
	£13,500	$\xleftarrow{\ =\ }$	£13,500	
June 10		£13,500 $\xrightarrow{\ =\ }$	NIL	£13,500
	£14,000	$\xleftarrow{\ =\ }$	£14,000	
August 31		£14,000 $\xrightarrow{\ =\ }$	NIL	£14,000
	£14,500	$\xleftarrow{\ =\ }$	£14,500	
November 20		£14,500 $\xrightarrow{\ =\ }$	NIL	£14,500
	£15,000	$\xleftarrow{\ =\ }$	£15,000	
Dec 15		£5,000 $\xrightarrow{\ =\ }$	£10,000	£5,000
	£5,000	$\xleftarrow{\ =\ }$	£15,000	

The *whole* of the stock is bought and sold 4 times, with about $\frac{1}{3}$ of the stock being sold in the last month. So the stock 'turns over' 4.3 times.

If you total the end column, you will see that the total cost of goods sold is £60,000.

Of course, stock doesn't quite move like this – it is being bought and sold all the time, not just 4.3 times a year, but it might help you to see it like this.

Generally, the faster stock turns over, the better, and money tied up in stock is not earning anything. In addition, stock is costly to store, insure and handle, and it may deteriorate or go out of fashion.

AJM is holding stock for about three months before selling it, which is quite slow, although this does depend on the type of business. A seller of cut flowers needs to turnover stock every day – 365 times a year – whereas an aircraft manufacturer will take much longer.

Debtors' collection period

This ratio tell us how many days debtors take to pay up.

$$\text{Debtor days} = \frac{\text{Debtors}}{\text{Credit sales}} \times 365$$

For AJM, the debtors' collection period is:

$$\frac{12,000}{100,000} \times 365 = 44 \text{ days}$$

Note – this is assuming that all sales are made on credit.

Whether this is good or bad depends on the type of business. The faster that debtors pay up, the quicker the business receives its money.

Creditors' payment period

This ratio tells us how many days we take to pay our creditors.

$$\text{Creditor days} = \frac{\text{Creditors}}{\text{Credit purchases}} \times 365$$

AJM's creditors' figure includes £3,000 for tax and dividends, so the true figure of creditors from whom goods have been purchased, is £19,000.

AJM's creditors' payment period is:

$$\frac{19,000}{62,000} \times 365 = 112 \text{ days}$$

The longer we take to pay our creditors, the longer we have the cash in our bank account. However, too long a period might antagonize the creditors. AJM is taking nearly four months to pay its creditors.

It is important to aim to pay creditors more slowly than customers pay us, to aid cash flow.

Fixed asset turnover

This measures how efficiently fixed assets are used to produce sales. The same ratio can be used on different groups of fixed assets, or on current assets.

$$\text{Fixed asset turnover} = \frac{\text{Turnover}}{\text{Fixed assets}}$$

For AJM, the fixed asset turnover is:

$$\frac{100,000}{77,000} = 1.3$$

This means that for every £1 invested in fixed assets, sales of £1.30 are achieved. The greater the ratio, the more 'productive' the fixed assets are considered to be. Businesses with heavy investment in fixed assets will experience a low rate of turnover. Businesses like that probably spend less money on labour and overheads.

Activity 17

From the following data, calculate four efficiency ratios:

	£
Opening stocks	20,000
Closing stocks	26,000
Cost of goods sold	74,000
Credit sales for the year	120,000
Credit purchases for the year	80,000
Fixed assets	40,000
Debtors	10,000
Creditors	8,000

See Feedback section for answer to this activity.

ANALYSING FINANCIAL STATEMENTS

Gearing ratio

This measures the proportion of finance which has been provided by long-term lenders, compared to other investors. There are several ways of calculating it. It is possible to include preference shareholders as long-term lenders, as they receive a fixed rate of dividend similar to the fixed rate of interest which lenders receive.

$$\text{Gearing ratio} = \frac{\text{Debt and fixed rate capital}}{\text{Equity capital}} \times 100$$

For AJM, there are no preference shares, so the gearing ratio is:

$$\frac{10,000}{90,000} \times 100 = 11\%$$

This indicates that the fixed-interest lenders provide only 11% of the sum provided by the shareholders. This is *low gearing*. A ratio of over 50% is *high gearing*. A highly geared company will have to earmark a substantial part of its profits in interest payments, which have to be paid. In times of recession, this could be a burden.

Security ratios

There are many of these, but most are beyond the level you need for your studies at the moment. Just one might be useful for you to know, which is the earnings per share (EPS) ratio. This shows how much profit the company has made which belongs to the ordinary shareholders. Remember, though, that although profit *belongs* to the shareholders, it does not necessarily mean that it will be paid out in dividends.

$$\text{Earnings per share} = \frac{\text{Net profit after tax}}{\text{Number of ordinary shares issued}}$$

Its earnings per share are:

$$\frac{8,000}{73,000} = £0.109 \text{ or } 11\text{p per share}$$

This is often compared to the EPS of other companies, so that investors can decide which is best.

Activity 18

From the following data, calculate the gearing ratio and earnings per share:

	£
Net profit after tax	12,000
Number of ordinary shares	180,000
Equity capital	240,000
Debts	80,000

See Feedback section for answer to this activity.

Interpreting the ratios

Calculating the ratios is only the starting point in analysing the accounts of a business.

Once that has been done, *comparison with other companies, previous periods or targets* is vital, so that a fuller picture can be obtained.

Look at the following ratios calculated for A. Firm Ltd, for two years.

	Year 1	**Year 2**
Gross profit margin	40%	50%
Net profit margin	10%	8%
Return on capital employed	6%	7%
Current ratio	2.2	2.8
Acid test ratio	1.0	0.7
Stock turnover	10 times	6 times
Debtors' collection period	40 days	30 days
Creditors' payment period	35 days	45 days
Gearing ratio	20%	60%
Earnings per share	5p	6p

Has the company improved in year 2?

Well, the answer is – yes and no! The gross profit margin has improved, but the net profit margin has decreased. This might be because sales have actually decreased in the second year, but improved purchasing methods have reduced the cost of sales by a greater amount. Many of the overheads will stay the same even though sales have decreased, and hence producing a lower net profit percentage on sales.

ANALYSING FINANCIAL STATEMENTS

However, the return on capital employed has improved, so shareholders might be happier. Earnings per share have also improved, giving shareholders greater comfort. But gearing has risen significantly, putting greater pressure on the profits and leaving less money for shareholders in the future.

The current ratio has increased, although 2.8 may be wasteful. Creditors might be happy with that increase. But the acid test ratio has fallen, which might have an adverse effect on creditors. This probably means that the current assets in year 2 contain a great deal of stock – which is borne out by the reduction in the rate of stock turnover. However, cash flow has been improved by collecting debtors more quickly, and slowing down the speed of payment to creditors. In year 1, the firm was paying its creditors faster than it was receiving the money in.

So, what is the conclusion from the above? Well, there isn't one. It all depends on who you are (an investor, a lender, an employee, a creditor, a factory manager, an office supervisor, etc.). It depends, too, on what you are looking for. An investor might be interested in a short-term return, in which case year 2 has improved, but in the long term, hefty interest payments may prevent that. And it depends on the reasons behind some of the changes. Stock might be awaiting a large order, or management might have anticipated a shortage. Trading expenses might have included a one-off advertising campaign which has not yet produced results.

Analysing financial statements is extremely difficult – as you can see!

Summary

Now that you have completed this chapter, you should be able to calculate a range of ratios for an organization and comment upon them. You should appreciate the usefulness and limitations of ratio analysis, and the importance of investigating changes in ratios before drawing conclusions.

You should know the main areas of comparison, which are performance, solvency, efficiency, gearing and security.

Review and discussion questions

1 What is a ratio?
2 As well as calculating ratios, what else should be done with them?
3 Consider an organization whose gross profit margin has improved, but its net profit margin has declined. What could be the reasons for these changes?
4 Is a high current ratio a good thing to have?
5 Why is it important to have a high rate of stock turnover?
6 What is meant by 'high gearing' and what are its effects?

Case study From the following set of accounts, produce a range of ratios, together with comments:

Trading and profit and loss account

	xxx1		xxx2	
	£000	£000	£000	£000
Sales		2,800		3,000
Less cost of sales:				
Opening stock	420		300	
Purchases	2,400		2,600	
	2,820		2,900	
Less closing stock	300		350	
		2,520		2,550
Gross profit		280		450
Less expenses		144		350
Net profit		136		100

Continued overleaf

ANALYSING FINANCIAL STATEMENTS

Balance sheet as at 31 December

	xxx1		xxx2	
	£000	£000	£000	£000
Fixed assets		1,200		1,300
Current assets				
Stocks	300		350	
Debtors	240		400	
Bank and cash	40		–	
	580		750	
Less Current liabilities				
Creditors	270		150	
Overdraft	–		300	
	270		450	
Net current assets		310		300
		1,510		1,600
Less Long-term liabilities		200		150
		1,310		1,450
Financed by:				
Capital at 1 January		1,174		1,350
Net profit		136		100
		1,310		1,450

In addition, you are told that at 1 January xxx1 debtors and creditors amounted to £160,000 and £250,000, respectively.

Work-based assignment

B1.1

Obtain the accounts of your own organization, or one in which you are interested. Calculate a range of ratios for a two-year period, and comment on your findings.

6 Cost control

Learning objectives

On completion of this chapter, you will be able to:

- understand the meaning of cost control
- classify costs into appropriate headings
- understand how costs behave in different situations
- understand the meaning of 'cost units' and the different types of cost units
- determine costs which can be *allocated* to cost centres or units
- calculate costs to be *apportioned* to cost centres
- understand how costs are *absorbed* into product/service costs

Introduction

Cost control is the means by which the costs incurred by an organization are identified, quantified, grouped together in an appropriate manner, and compared with planned limits. This comparison is intended to give management the information they require to determine the effectiveness of their operations, and to enable them to make decisions.

There are many different techniques of cost control, suited to different situations. There is no one 'best' technique, and it is probably fair to say that none is perfect, especially in today's rapidly changing and complex business environment. In the past, organizations generally concentrated on the provision of only a few products or services, made up mainly of materials and/or labour costs, and simple techniques of cost control were quite satisfactory. Nowadays, however, organizations incur costs in a much wider variety of areas, such as marketing, human resources, research and development, information technology, training and supervision. This has resulted in the 'old' costing techniques being rather too simplistic, and consequently new techniques are being developed.

However, there are still many basic principles involved in costing, which we will examine in this chapter.

What are costs?

Costs are amounts incurred in the provision of goods and services. Ultimately, an organization will want to determine the cost of each individual product or service (or groups of products and services) which it provides, but in doing so it will often need to calculate the costs of other activities which it undertakes and which help in the provision of its goods and services.

For example, a furniture maker will incur costs in the wood, varnish, glue, etc. which go into a piece of furniture. There will also be labour costs, and the cost of using machinery to make the items. These are often quite straightforward to determine. Let us suppose that these costs amount to £100 for a table. But there will be other ancillary costs incurred in running the business, which add to the overall cost of the table, such as telephone charges, rent and rates, insurance, supervisors' wages, marketing, distribution, warehousing, running the accounts department, and so on. These costs all need to be considered in determining the overall costs of the table – and eventually its selling price.

You can see that if he sells the table for £101, he may well have insufficient money to pay for all the other costs he incurs.

Activity 19

Look at your own organization, or one with which you are familiar. What are its products and services? What are the *main* costs which go into its provision? List the *ancillary* costs which the organization also incurs.

See Feedback section for answer to this activity.

Cost classification

Before you can start to collect costs together, it is important that you are able to classify costs into particular types. There are many different ways of doing this. If you consider your own personal expenditure, you might classify the costs into 'essential' and 'non-essential' or 'long-term' and 'short-term'. Some costs remain the same no matter what you do – your car tax for example is fixed by the government, is unavoidable, and remains the same irrespective of the number of miles you travel. Petrol, on the other hand, increases the more miles you travel – and it can be avoided by travelling less!

There are several 'standard' ways of classifying costs, which are used both separately and together in different situations.

The elements of cost

One way of classifying costs is to group them into one of three main headings:

1 materials costs
2 labour costs
3 expenses

Material costs are the components, assemblies, fabrics, liquids, consumables, etc. which an organization uses. It includes raw materials not yet processed in any way, partly finished items (often called 'work in progress'), completed goods ready for sale, packing materials, stationery, cleaning materials, etc.

Labour costs are the costs incurred in employing the staff, and includes not only their normal wages, but also overtime payments, pensions contributions, employers' national insurance, profit sharing costs, etc.

Expenses includes all the other costs of the organization – the list is enormous. Examples are the cost of premises, administration, marketing, delivery, finance charges, research, maintenance of equipment, cleaning, training and personnel functions.

Direct and indirect costs

This classification is used to distinguish between those costs which can be directly identified with a particular product, batch of products, service, job or activity, and those which cannot. One way of determining whether or not a cost is direct is to to ask the question 'would it still be incurred if that particular product or activity did not exist?'. If the answer is 'no', then it is a direct cost.

Direct costs are usually only identified with goods or services which provide income. In a manufacturing organization, this would be the products sold. In a service organization, it would be the service provided – for example, in a school, the teacher's salary would be a direct cost of teaching a particular class. It follows that a direct cost must be able to be accurately measured against the product or the service, e.g. as an hourly rate.

Indirect costs are all the other costs which cannot be directly identified with a particular product.

Both direct and indirect costs can also be classified into *materials, labour and expenses.*

Direct materials would include the materials which form part of the product or batch of products. *Indirect materials* would include things such as lubricating oils, stationery, cleaning materials, spare parts, etc.

Direct labour would include the labour costs of workers making the products or providing the services. *Indirect labour* would include the costs of supervision, administration, management, storekeeping, etc.

Direct expenses are relatively uncommon. Some examples include the hire of tools for a particular job, royalties payable for the use of a special design, import duties on the purchase of materials. Most expenses are *indirect expenses.*

Indirect materials, labour and expenses are also collectively called *overheads.* They are often grouped according to the main activities of the organization, e.g. production, selling and administration overheads.

Prime cost

The prime cost of a product or service is the total of its direct materials, labour and expenses.

Activity 20

Complete the following table for each item of expenditure incurred in a company which designs and prints stationery.

Item of expenditure	Materials, labour or expenses?	Direct or indirect?
Salaries of office staff		
Printing inks		
Repairs to machinery		
Printer's wage		
Paper costs		
Telephone costs		
Fee to design artist		
Insurance		
Cleaning materials		
Rent and rates		

Cost behaviour

Yet another classification of costs is by the way in which they behave in changing circumstances. Some costs remain steady irrespective of the level of activity – do you remember the example given earlier of car tax remaining the same however many miles you travel, whereas petrol costs increase with greater distances?

Those were examples of *fixed costs* and *variable costs*.

Fixed costs

These are costs which remain the same irrespective of changes in the level of activity (see Figure 6.1a). Examples include insurance, rent and rates. Only significant changes in activity

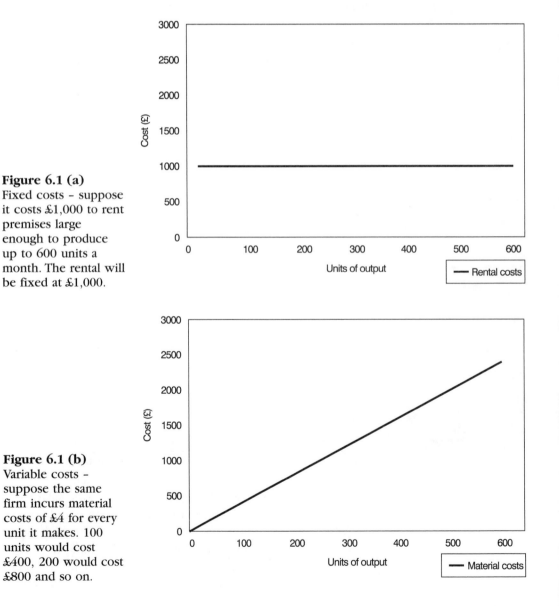

Figure 6.1 (a)
Fixed costs – suppose it costs £1,000 to rent premises large enough to produce up to 600 units a month. The rental will be fixed at £1,000.

Figure 6.1 (b)
Variable costs – suppose the same firm incurs material costs of £4 for every unit it makes. 100 units would cost £400, 200 would cost £800 and so on.

will cause these costs to alter, but more minor changes will have no effect. That is not to say that these costs never change at all – inflation and other factors will cause them to rise or fall, but not in proportion to the level of activity.

Variable costs

These are costs which change *in direct proportion to the level of activity* (see Figure 6.1b). For example, if one more unit is produced, there will be an increase in costs. If production increases by five per cent, variable costs will increase by five per cent.

Direct costs are almost always variable, whereas indirect costs rarely are. It is common to find direct labour classed as variable. However, in most organizations, direct labour is not strictly variable – it does not vary *in direct proportion to* the level of activity. So, a worker might be paid £250 a week, and normally produces 100 units. If he produces only 90 units one week, unless he is paid on a strict 'units of output' basis, it is likely that he will still be paid £250. Even employees paid on a 'units of output' basis often have a basic wage to protect them from unacceptably low wages when the level of production is outside their control – e.g. if a machine breaks down.

However, you will be asked to regard direct labour as variable in the examples used in this book.

Semi-variable or semi-fixed costs

There are costs which contain a fixed element and a variable element (see Figure 6.1c). An example is the cost of telephones, which comprise a fixed rental charge, plus a variable charge based on the number and length of calls made.

Stepped costs

These are costs which are fixed up to a certain level, but which change suddenly once that level is exceeded (see Figure 6.1d). An example might be supervisors' salaries. A single supervisor might supervise between three and six employees, but if the number of employees rises to eight, a second supervisor might be required. Another example is a doctor's practice. A single doctor might look after up to 2,000 patients. If a new housing estate is built, attracting 200 new

Figure 6.1 (c)
Semi-variable costs –
suppose the firm pays
£1,000 a month to
hire a delivery
vehicle, and £1 for
every unit
transported. 100 units
would cost £1,100
(£1,000 + £100), 200
units would cost
£1,200 and so on

Figure 6.1 (d)
Stepped costs –
suppose it costs
£1,000 to hire
machinery to produce
up to 200 units. If
201 units are
produced, another
machine is needed,
and a third machine if
over 400 units are
produced

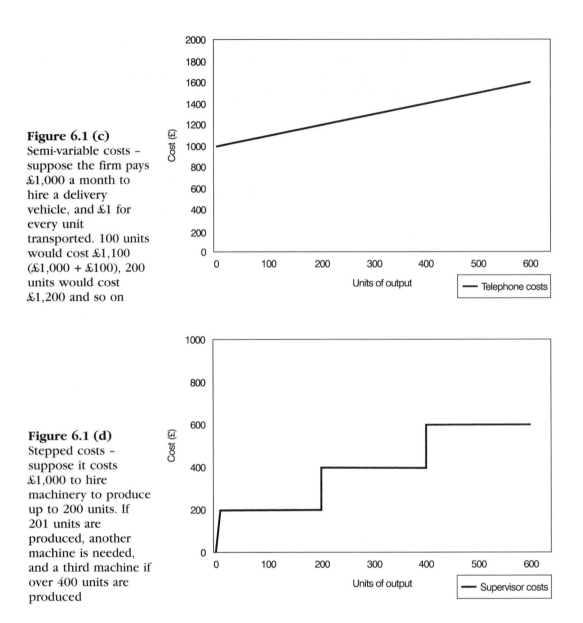

people, a second doctor is required – and suddenly the cost of patient care has doubled for an increase in workload of only ten per cent.

There will be an opportunity for you to see the effects of the different cost behaviours in the next chapter.

Investigate 8

Identify three examples of each of fixed, variable, semi-fixed and stepped costs which occur in your own organization.

In practice, it is extremely difficult to put costs into such clear-cut 'pockets', so if you found that you struggled with the classification of some items, do not worry. The accountant probably has the same difficulty, which is one of the reasons why costing techniques are less than perfect!

Cost units

The end result of the costing process is to determine the cost of a particular cost *unit*. The cost unit will vary in different organizations, and there may be several different cost units in a single organization. For example, in a hospital, the main cost units will be based on patients – costs could be calculated for each patient, each night or each operation. In determining these costs, the hospital will also have to calculate other costs such as the cost for each consulting hour, the cost of each patient meal, the cost of an x-ray or a general anaesthetic.

These are all *cost units*.

Cost centres

A cost centre is a 'collecting point' for the costs of a particular location, function, activity, type of expense or asset, whose costs are part of the overall cost of the provision of goods and services. Costs are gathered together in these cost centres as a starting point in the costing process. Examples of cost centres include:

- a production department
- a machine or group of machines
- a sales team
- a store room
- a personnel department
- a computer department
- premises costs, e.g. electricity, insurance, rent, maintenance
- a fleet of vehicles

Once the costs have been collected in a cost centre, they can then be used to calculate the cost of a unit – so in the list above, the cost centre for a fleet of vehicles could be used to find the cost per vehicle, or even the cost per mile travelled.

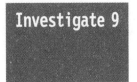

Investigate 9

Look at your own organization again. List some of the cost centres you think it might have.

Check your answers back at work – your accounting department should have a comprehensive list for you to look at. Which cost centre do your own activities come under?

Cost allocation

There are many different systems for collecting together the costs incurred. Computerized systems are much faster than manual systems and can cope with a greater number of cost centres and cost units. Many organizations use code numbers to group similar items together. For example, the code for head office might be '1'. The computer department might be coded '8'. Wages and salaries might be coded '4'. Overtime pay might be coded '7'.

Thus, overtime paid to a computer assistant at head office would be coded 1847. This would ensure that the cost is charged to the correct cost centre and can be easily identified.

This charging of expenditure to a particular cost centre or unit is known as *cost allocation*. As the costs are incurred, for example when invoices or timesheets are received, they are coded directly to the cost centre concerned.

Most direct costs can be easily allocated to their cost units. It is the indirect costs which cause most difficulty. They are usually only able to be allocated to cost centres rather than cost units, and some require further analysis in order to determine which cost centres should be charged with their cost.

Cost apportionment

Some costs cannot be identified with a specific cost centre, but need to be shared out between several cost centres. An example of such a cost is rates. Obviously, when the rates bill is received it may well be coded to a 'miscellaneous property expenses' cost centre. Later on, it is *apportioned* between the cost centres which share that cost, e.g. to the production, marketing, computer and administration department cost centres.

The method of apportionment of such costs should be done as carefully as possible. The basis of apportionment should be chosen to reflect a fair and equitable proportion of the cost being charged to each cost centre. A common basis for the apportionment of property costs, such as rates, is *floor area*.

<table>
<tr><td>**Example**</td><td>

Suppose a catering college has a total floor area of 14,000 square metres, split as follows:

Classrooms	6,000 square metres
Teaching restaurant	2,000 square metres
Library	3,000 square metres
Student refectory	2,000 square metres
Offices	1,000 square metres

The total rates bill for the year is £70,000. This would be apportioned on the basis of floor area, by dividing the total bill by the total floor area to find a cost per square metre.

Total bill £70,000, divided by 14,000 square metres = £5 per square metre

Each department is then charged with their portion of the cost:

Classrooms	6,000 × £5 = £30,000
Teaching restaurant	2,000 × £5 = £10,000
Library	3,000 × £5 = £15,000
Student refectory	2,000 × £5 = £10,000
Offices	1,000 × £5 = £ 5,000
Total bill apportioned	£70,000

</td></tr>
<tr><td>**Activity 21**</td><td>

An organization has the following employees in each of its departments:

Sales and marketing	14 employees
Accounts	8 employees
Payroll	4 employees
Purchasing	10 employees
Research	3 employees
Production	21 employees
Total	60 employees

The total cost of the staff canteen is £18,000. Calculate the amount to be apportioned to each of the above departments, based on the number of employees in each.

See Feedback section for answer to this activity.

</td></tr>
</table>

COST CONTROL

It is important to realize that the above process of cost apportionment is not very precise. The staff in the production department might use the canteen far more often than, say, the research staff, so the apportionment of cost may well be inequitable. If systems can be devised to be more accurate and fair than this method, then they should be, but often the cost of developing them outweighs the benefits to be gained.

Activity 22

Look at the following list of overheads which need to be apportioned between cost centres. Can you suggest a reasonable basis for each of them?

    Rent
    Heating
    Equipment insurance
    Training department costs
    Computer department costs
    Health and safety

See Feedback section for answer to this activity.

Overhead absorption

The overall aim of the costing system is to determine the cost of individual products and services. Once the costs of the production department (using the example of a manufacturing organization as being the most complex type of organization to cost) have been determined, through allocation and apportionment, then the costs of the supporting service departments (administration, etc.) are also apportioned to the production department. The production department cost centres then contain all the costs of the organization.

A production department might make several different products. Their direct costs can be *allocated* to the costs units quite easily, but overheads cannot. These need to be *absorbed* into the individual products on some basis.

A common basis in the past has been that of *time*, either machine time or labour time. This is because many overheads occur on a time basis – buildings insurance, rent, rates, etc. are all charged for a period of a year, so are not based on the level of activity or the value of the items being produced.

Take a production deparment with total overheads of £12,000 a year. It produces five different products, each requiring differing amounts of time to produce on a machine. There is only one machine, which operates for forty hours a week, fifty weeks of the year – that's 2,000 hours. The overhead cost per machine hour is therefore:

£12,000 divided by 2,000 hours = £6 per machine hour

Each product can then *absorb* its own share of overheads based on machine hours. So if product A takes five hours to produce, it absorbs £30 of overheads. Product B, taking three hours, absorbs only £18 of overheads.

Activity 23

A firm of solicitors, comprising four partners, expects to spend about seventy-five per cent of its time on client matters, totalling 120 hours per week. Overheads for a week in June are expected to be £1,500. A new client asks for a quote for a job taking ten hours to be done during June. The direct costs are anticipated to be £30 per hour. Calculate a quote for the job, assuming that a profit of £200 is required.

See Feedback section for answer to this activity.

The whole of the costing process can be shown in Figure 6.2.

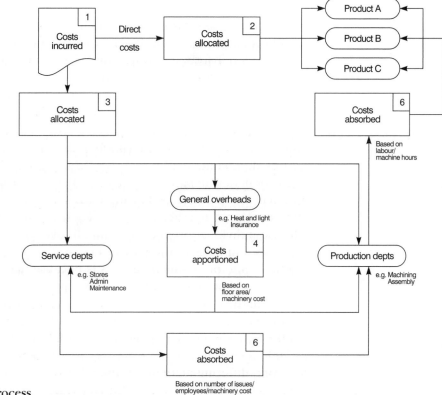

Figure 6.2
The costing process

Summary

Now that you have completed this chapter, you should appreciate the meaning of cost control. You should be able to classify costs in various ways according to the circumstances, and understand how costs change in response to changes in the level of activity. You should understand the meaning of 'cost units' and 'cost centres' and be able to determine costs which can be allocated to cost units/centres as opposed to those which need to be apportioned. You should be able to calculate the cost of a product or service using appropriate methods of apportionment and absorption of overheads.

Review and discussion questions

1 What is the purpose of cost control?
2 A manufacturing organization has several ways in which costs can be classified. Identify three methods of cost classification and discuss the possible applications of each in a manufacturing situation.
3 What do you understand by the terms 'cost units' and 'cost centres'. How do they differ from each other? Give two examples of each.
4 There are several different bases of apportioning overheads to cost centres. Choose five overhead costs and suggest a reasonable basis for the apportionment of each.
5 In groups, consider the statement that 'overhead costs should be absorbed into the cost of products on the basis of the materials cost of each item'.

Case study

ABC Limited is a manufacturer of shoes. Direct materials consist of leather, plastics and lining materials. Shoes are manufactured in batches of 50 pairs at a time, before changing the tooling on the machinery to produce a different style. Direct labour consists of machine operators with a supervisor over every ten machines. The company has a large factory, supplemented by a warehouse, canteen, offices and computer suite. The offices house the marketing, personnel and accounts departments, while the factory houses the research team and the purchasing department.

Identify the cost units and possible cost centres which might exist in the above company. What types of costs do you envisage the company incurring and how would you suggest allocating and apportioning these costs to arrive at the cost of a single pair of shoes?

RESOURCES MANAGEMENT

Case study

You have just been appointed as team leader to a team of twelve care workers in your local authority. The carers go out to the homes of the sick and elderly every morning, lunchtime and evening. Some clients receive three visits a day, others two or only one visit. Each visit lasts for an hour. The carers help the clients to get washed and dressed, prepare meals, take their prescribed drugs, and generally assist in their well being. The total time taken by the carers is 168 hours per week.

Each carer provides his or her own car, and receives a mileage allowance of 40p per mile. The carers are paid £3 per hour for their time, excluding travelling. The total mileage bill for the month is expected to be £1,344.

You are based in an office at the town hall with a floor area of 16 square metres. You spend most of your day there, on the telephone and carrying out administrative duties. You are paid £12,000 per year, and other benefits, pension contributions, etc. cost the local authority a further £1,200 a year. The town hall floor area totals 2,400 square metres, and the premises running costs are £720,000 per annum.

Calculate the cost for an hourly visit to a client.

Work-based assignment

B1.1
B1.2

Investigate the costing systems in use at your place of work. Produce a report (of about 1,500 words), outlining the following items:

• the cost units involved
• the coding system used
• the costs which are *allocated* to cost units and/or cost centres
• the method(s) of apportioning overheads to other cost centres
• the overhead absorption methods and rates used

Comment on the suitability of each of the methods you have outlined.

7 Budgets

Learning objectives

By the end of this chapter you will be able to:

- appreciate the purpose and use of budgets
- understand how budgets are compiled
- identify the principal budget factor
- prepare a variety of budgets for sales and production
- use budgets to identify variances
- appreciate the need for further investigation into variances

Introduction

A budget is a formal, quantitative statement of the resources required for carrying out activities over a period of time.

An organization might prepare budgets for any of its activities including the following:

- sales
- production
- expenses
- materials requirements
- labour requirements
- capital expenditure
- machine time
- training costs
- cash
- research costs

and many more.

In addition, it will probably bring them all together into a forecast profit and loss account and balance sheet. This chapter looks at the different types of budget, what they contain and how they are prepared. It considers where the data for budgets comes from, and equally important, what happens to budgets once they have been prepared, and how they assist in the monitoring and control of an organization's activities.

The budget period

The period of time is usually fairly short – a long-range plan is called a *forecast*. The period might be as long as a year, or as short as a month. Most annual budgets are broken down into months.

The purpose of budgeting

A budget is the standard by which future performance is measured. It aims to establish clear and unambiguous standards of performance.

If there is no budget, there is no way of knowing whether the performance of an organization is acceptable or not. A budget is the only way of expressing the objectives of the organization in monetary terms.

There are several purposes of budgets:

- to ensure that the objectives of the organization are met
- to force managers to plan and look ahead
- to set targets for performance
- to act as a motivating force
- to encourage the communication of ideas
- to co-ordinate activities so that there is no duplication of work, and no important areas are omitted
- to establish areas of responsibility
- to provide a system of comparison and control

The psychology of budgets

For a budget to perform any of the functions above, it must be acceptable to those who use it. This means that it must have been discussed and agreed with those who are going to be responsible for its implementation. Preferably, those people should be involved with its production.

The targets set by a budget should be fair and achievable. Budgets which are out of reach only act as demotivators. On the other hand, budgets which are too easily attainable do not encourage efficiency. Following on from this, budgets must be amended if circumstances change, as an out-of-date budget is of no use.

The budget must be used. A budget, however carefully prepared, is of no use if it is filed away and forgotten. It must be compared with the actual results on a regular basis, and be seen as an important tool of monitoring and control.

Those using the budget must fully understand how it is made up, what it contains, and what its purpose is. They must appreciate the importance of adhering to the budget and of achieving the budgeted levels. It must be expressed in terms which the users understand, backed up with additional information if necessary. Budgets are often prepared in summary form, but there must be the facility to provide further detail and breakdown as required.

The budget must not be seen as a straightjacket, to be adhered to at all costs, irrespective of the circumstances. If additional expenditure is required which will produce a reduction in unit costs, then it should not be dismissed purely because it has not been included in the budget.

Comparison of budgeted figures with actual should not be seen as an exercise to apportion blame, otherwise people will be afraid of the budget. It should be seen as an opportunity for control and adjustment, so as to improve performance. Variances from budget should be properly investigated so as to avoid incorrect assumptions being drawn.

Gathering data for budgets

Much of the data for budgets is internal to the organization. For example, data on production, sales, marketing, personnel, research and development will come from the organization's own costing and financial systems. Not all of the data will be in written format; some will be held electronically or visually, some will be informal, e.g. held in people's minds. External data will be required to some extent, even for short-term budgets, such as data on the economy, competitors, the extent of the market, etc.

The principal budget factor

It is possible to produce a detailed budget for almost every area of an organization. Such budgets are known as subsidiary budgets and often they have to be produced first before other budgets can be produced. However, in most organizations the starting point for the preparation of budgets is to determine the principal budget factor or key factor. This is the item on which all the other budgets are based and take their figures from. The most common principal budget factor is sales, but it is not always the case that sales are achievable – it might be that productive capacity, shortage of materials or skilled labour can restrict the level of sales. In a service organization, the principal budget factor might be the available labour hours, while in a local authority it might be a planned reduction in expenditure as dictated by the government.

The sales budget

If sales is the key factor, then the sales budget is the first to be produced. It will be based on the number of units to be sold, and the expected selling price. Ideally, it should be broken down into individual products or product categories, and perhaps also into geographical areas. It should consider the timing of sales, e.g. seasonal variations, and should be broken down into short periods rather than whole years.

It is important that the starting point for budget preparation should be carefully thought out. To simply use last year's budget and add a straight five per cent to everything is totally inappropriate and unreasonable. It is likely that some market research will be needed to produce a realistic sales budget.

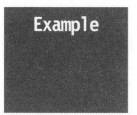

The sales budget for your firm for the next year contains the following figures for January, February and March.

	Jan	Feb	March	Quarter
Number of units	1,200	1,400	1,000	3,600
Sales at £40 each	£48,000	£56,000	£40,000	£144,000

Production budgets

These usually follow the sales budgets, and are also prepared by product and period. There will be individual budgets prepared for materials used, materials purchased, labour and overheads, as well as budgets for machine utilization. These budgets will consider the level of output, materials usage and cost, labour efficiency, wage rates including overtime and bonuses, and the absorption of overheads. You are not going to cover all of these budgets in this book as their preparation is mainly undertaken by cost accountants, but the more important ones will help you to appreciate the importance of, and difficulties involved in, budgeting.

The production volume budget

Some organizations like to maintain an even flow of production, i.e produce the same quantity each week/month. This makes production planning easier and is more acceptable to the work force. However, if the level of sales is not even, then it does mean that there will be stocks of finished goods on hand at the end of some months, and the firm will need to make sure it does not run out of goods.

Using the sales figures for your firm above, you can see that 3,600 units are required for the whole of the first quarter. But if you produce an even flow of 1,200 units per month, you will be 200 units short in February. Therefore you will need to produce more than this or keep a stock on hand.

Alternatively, if the firm can produce different amounts each month, by paying overtime or engaging part-time staff, the production can more easily mirror the sales level, perhaps with a smaller amount of stock on hand for emergencies.

Example

Using the sales figures from the sales budget in the previous section, and assuming that the firm starts with a stock of goods of 250 units, the production budget might be as follows:

Production budget for March quarter (in units)

	Jan	Feb	Mar
Opening stock of goods	250	250	50
Production	1,200	1,200	1,200
	1,450	1,450	1,250
Sales	1,200	1,400	1,000
Closing stock of goods	250	50	250

The stock falls to 50 units at the end of February – management need to consider whether this is safe, or whether additional units should be made in February.

Activity 24

Produce a production budget for KK Limited for the months of January, February and March. Opening stock of finished goods is 300 units. Production will be 800 units per month, and sales will be 700 units in January, 600 units in February and 650 units in March. Comment on your results.

See Feedback section for answer to this activity.

The raw materials budget

Having decided on the monthly production, your firm now needs to make sure that it has enough raw materials to produce that quantity. Suppose that each unit takes 2 kilos of material – you need to make sure that you have 2,400 kilos available for each of the above months. It is probably also advisable to keep a stock on hand. And as with production, you need to decide whether to purchase an even quantity each month, or different amounts as required, or even place a bulk order in January in order to take advantage of bulk discounts. Your decision will take into account how and when you are going to pay for the materials, as well as other factors such as reliability of supply, quality of material, etc.

Other production budgets

Budgets will also be prepared for the purchasing of materials, the availability of labour and machinery, and overheads.

Converting quantity budgets into value budgets

The production budgets are initially prepared in terms of quantities – number of units, weight of materials, hours of labour, etc. These need to be converted to monetary values.

These values are brought together in the *Production cost budget*. Using the example from above, of production of 1,200 units per month, and the following information:

Each unit requires 2 kilos of material, costing £3 per kilo
1 hour of labour, costing £4 per hour
5 hours of machine time, costing £1 per hour

The production cost budget for the quarter would be:

	Jan	Feb	Mar	Total
	£	£	£	£
Materials	7,200	7,200	7,200	21,600
Labour	4,800	4,800	4,800	14,400
Machine time	6,000	6,000	6,000	18,000
Total cost	18,000	18,000	18,000	54,000

BUDGETS

Activity 25

Each unit of production in KK Limited takes 2 hours of direct labour, costing £4 per hour, and absorbs £3 of overheads. Materials cost is £2 per unit. Prepare a production cost budget for January, February and March. Production is 800 units a month.

See Feedback section for answer to this activity.

The purchases and sales budgets are then used to determine payments to creditors (suppliers) and receipts from debtors (customers), for the cash budget which was covered in Chapter 3.

Administration and overhead budgets

Separate budgets will be prepared for all other areas of the business such as marketing, office salaries, heat and light, depreciation, personnel and training.

Investigate 10

Obtain one or more budgets which your organization prepares. Where do the figures come from? Who uses them? What action is taken after they are prepared?

Capital expenditure budgets

These are prepared to show planned expenditure on capital items (fixed assets), e.g. buildings, plant and equipment, motor vehicles, office machinery, etc. There may also be a budget for unplanned expenditure during the year. Capital expenditure also includes major alterations to existing fixed assets. Smaller amounts of capital expenditure might be delegated to departmental or section managers, and even as a team leader you might have an allowance in your budget for some items. Larger amounts of capital expenditure might be controlled by a committee of senior managers, or even by the board of directors.

Some capital expenditure budgets might extend over several years, with planned expenditure broken down into annual periods.

The control of capital expenditure budgets over long periods is very complex as it often entails several different types of expenditure. The construction of a building, for example, would include costs for surveyors, architects, lawyers, accountants, builders, etc.

RESOURCES MANAGEMENT

Some capital items might be constructed by the organization's own labour, in which case there needs to be careful control over the calculation of materials, labour and overheads within the capital budget, and regular comparison of budgeted and actual figures to ensure that any potential overspend is recognized as early as possible.

The master budget

All the subsidiary budgets are brought together in a set of master budgets which will include a budgeted trading and profit and loss account and balance sheet.

Responsibilities for budgets

You can see that preparing budgets is a considerable task, involving a large number of people in different areas. Individual managers will be responsible for the budgets which cover their areas of control, assisted by their team leaders. They will be involved in the detailed calculations needed to arrive at accurate quantities and values, and will have to justify their conclusions.

Larger organizations will have a *budget committee*, comprising senior managers. The committee will have overall responsibility for co-ordinating the individual budgets. Once the budgets have been drawn up, and the overall picture is revealed, the budget committee will probably request that amendments are made. It might be that there is insufficient cash to finance the purchase of materials in a particular month. This might mean that the materials budget has to be amended, and consequently the production budget – and indeed perhaps all other budgets which follow on from there. Or additional vehicles and drivers might be required for the delivery of finished goods, with consequent amendments to those budgets.

The budget committee will also negotiate with individual budget managers where necessary, especially where budgeted expenditure is higher than the organization can accommodate.

Investigate 11 Identify who is responsible for the budgets of different areas within your organization. Make a list of individuals and their areas of responsibility.

BUDGETS

Budget changes

A budget is not a rigid structure, but exists as a guideline for monitoring and action. If circumstances change, then the budget should be changed accordingly. Actual results should be compared with a budget which reflects the same level of activity and set of circumstances otherwise the exercise is meaningless. It is rather like comparing your own expenditure with that of a millionaire - there is no comparison!

Some areas of a budget are more sensitive to change than others. Those which reflect variable activities, e.g. variable costs, are sensitive to changes in the level of activity; interest payable is sensitive to changes in national interest rates; wages are sensitive to national insurance contribution changes. These areas must be reviewed regularly to ensure that they are still accurate and representative of the current situation.

It is important to realize that a change to one budget will have an impact on other budgets. For example, if the level of sales changes this will affect other budgets which depend on sales - probably all of them, but especially production budgets and the cash budget.

Minor amendments to budgets can probably be absorbed fairly easily and dealt with by individual managers, but more major amendments should be referred back to the budget committee for consideration and approval.

Using budgets for monitoring and control

Budgets should not be produced and forgotten, but they are there to be used to monitor the actual performance of the organization, and to take action wherever necessary. To assist in this, various budgetary control reports are likely to be produced for every area of the organization, to show the budgeted and actual results, and the differences, both for the current month and for the year to date. As well as actual figures, percentages are often also included. These reports need to be prepared on a regular basis, so that action can be taken before too much time has elapsed; on the other hand, reports which are prepared too frequently can be misleading.

Variances

A variance is the difference between the budgeted figures and the actual figures. It can be either of the following:

- favourable
- unfavourable

A favourable variance is one which occurs when the actual figures show more revenue, or less cost, than was budgeted.

An unfavourable, or 'adverse' variance, occurs when the actual figures show less revenue, or more cost, than was budgeted.

Once the budgetary control report has been produced, the variances identified should be investigated further to determine their causes.

Budgets are prepared for a particular level of planned activity. If that level of activity is actually achieved, then it is sensible to compare the actual results with the budget.

Example

Your firm budgets to sell 1,000 units in July, for £20 each. It expects each unit to cost £3 in direct materials, £6 in direct labour, and £2 in variable expenses. Fixed costs are budgeted at £5,000. The actual results show that the target of 1,000 units was achieved, but total sales were £19,500, direct materials cost £2,400, direct labour cost £6,200, variable expenses were £1,900 and fixed costs were £5,100. A comparison of budget with actual can be made as follows:

	Budget £	Actual £	Variance £
Sales	20,000	19,500	500 A
Direct materials	3,000	2,400	600 F
Direct labour	6,000	6,200	200 A
Variable expenses	2,000	1,900	100 F
Fixed costs	5,000	5,100	100 A
Total costs	16,000	15,600	400 F
Profit	4,000	3,900	100 A

At first sight, it might seem that the budget has been almost met. The profit is only £100 short of the budget. It might be tempting to say that this is a minor difference and can be ignored. However, this small difference is masking some larger differences which are worthy of investigation. Sales were £500 below budget, and direct materials were £600 below budget. These are quite significant differences when you consider that the quantity sold was on target. Why should sales fall by so much? Why did materials cost so much less?

Activity 26

Prepare a budget statement such as the one shown earlier, which compares the original budget with the actual results, from the following data:

Budget data per unit	selling price £30
	direct materials £14
	direct labour £6
	variable expenses £3

| Budgeted fixed costs | £8,000 |

| Budgeted quantity | 2,000 |

Actual results	sales, 2000 units at £32 each
	direct materials £30,000
	direct labour £11,500
	variable expenses £5,000
	fixed costs £8,600

See Feedback section for answer to this activity.

Investigating variances

All variances should be investigated. At this stage in your studies, you are not going to consider some of the more advanced techniques of variance investigation, but you should be aware of the possibilities. Even a 'nil' variance should be investigated. It does not necessarily mean that everything went according to plan. For example, you might have budgeted for 1,000 kg of material at £3 per kg, and actually used £1,500 kg at £2 per kg. the variance would be nil, as both would produce a total materials cost of £3,000. It would be tempting to ignore the variance of nil, but in fact it does not necessarily mean that everything has gone according to plan.

Reasons for variances

The above variances need to be investigated to determine why they have occurred. In this example, one thing is certain - they have not occurred because of the level of activity - this is exactly as was budgeted. There must be other reasons.

- **Sales revenue**

The only possible explanation for an unfavourable variance is that the selling price was lowered. This might have been to take account of market forces, to remain competitive, or to try to increase the level of sales – which did not seem to work.

- **Direct materials**

There are two obvious explanations for a favourable variance. These are:

- the purchase price of materials has fallen
- the efficiency with which materials are used has improved

But even these are not certain. There could be various combinations of factors which produce a lower total materials cost. It might be that a higher price has been paid for materials, but due to better quality, the level of wastage has decreased.

Or it might be that a lower price has been paid for materials, and the level of wastage has remained the same – or even increased.

All are worthy of further investigation.

Labour

The actual cost of labour is £200 more than budgeted. This could be due to:

- an increase in wages
- a decrease in efficiency of the work force

or some combination of the two.

It might be that five workers were expected to produce 200 units a month each. But the actual situation might have been four workers producing 250 units a month each. Both would result in 1,000 units a month being produced – which agrees with the budget. But in order to encourage those four workers to produce more, it might have been necessary to pay overtime rates or bonuses, so the overall cost per hour would increase.

Again, investigation is worthwhile.

Suppose that a firm budgets to make 5,000 units from 15,000 kg of material costing £1 per kilogram, and it actually pays £18,000 for materials. Why do you think this might be?

See Feedback section for answer to this activity.

Variable expenses

The same possibilities might apply to variable expenses.

Fixed costs

Fixed costs are slightly different in that they are less controllable than variable costs, and much depends on the method of apportionment.

In the above example, fixed costs were £100 more than budget. This might be because fixed costs were higher than expected, or it might be that the number of machine hours, on which fixed costs are apportioned, was greater than expected.

You can see that further investigation is needed into all of these areas to obtain a full picture.

Flexible budgets

The above example is relevant only when the actual level of activity is the same as the budgeted level of activity. If the two are different, then a different approach needs to be taken.

Look at the example of a household. Imagine that in your household there are two people. You draw up a budget for the next twelve months on that basis. But early in the year, two more people join your household – long-lost children who have decided to return now that they are unemployed and penniless. Consider the original budget:

	£
Income (2 × £10,000)	20,000
Food, clothes, travel, etc.	8,000
Mortgage, insurance	4,000
Heat, light and telephone	2,000
Entertainment	1,000
Total costs	15,000
Surplus	5,000

Now we have two extra people, the actual income and expenditure is as follows:

	£
Income (with state benefits)	25,000
Food, clothes, travel, etc.	16,000
Mortgage, insurance	4,000
Heat, light and telephone	3,000
Entertainment	2,000
Total costs	25,000
Surplus	NIL

At first examination, it seems that the family budget has collapsed. Well, not surprising. There are two extra people. If we are using the budget for control purposes, then we need to consider what changes we could expect in the budget now that there are four people instead of two. The budgeted surplus of £5,000 has disappeared. Is this reasonable? Or should we expect a surplus still? Or even a deficit?

The point is that it is meaningless to compare the original budget for two people, with the actual results for four. Oh, it is a useful exercise in making you depressed, but if you are facing facts, you need to know what the expectation is when there are two extra people in the house.

Only then, can you determine whether expenditure has been controlled or not.

A 'flexible budget' attempts to overcome this difficulty.

Example

Take the example we looked at earlier and compare the budget with actual results, assuming a level of activity of 1,500 units.

Your firm budgets to sell 1,000 units in July, for £20 each. It expects each unit to cost £3 in direct materials, £6 in direct labour, and £2 in variable expenses. Fixed costs are budgeted at £5,000. The actual results show that sales of £1,500 units was achieved, with total sales of £29,250, direct materials cost £3,600, direct labour cost £9,300, variable expenses were £2,850 and fixed costs were £5,100. A comparison of budget with actual can be made as follows:

BUDGETS

	Budget £	**Actual** £	**Variance** £
Sales	20,000	29,250	9,250 F
Direct materials	3,000	3,600	600 A
Direct labour	6,000	9,300	3,300 A
Variable expenses	2,000	2,850	850 A
Fixed costs	5,000	5,100	100 A
Total costs	16,000	20,850	4,850 F
Profit	4,000	8,400	4,400 F

Do you think it is reasonable to compare a budget for 1,000 units with an actual level of activity of 1,500 units? You would expect sales, and most costs, to be higher than the original budget. As they are in the above example. The end result is that profit was £4,400 higher than budget. Well, that can't be bad, can it? But is it as high as it should have been?

Any comparison of budget and actual results would be distorted by the fact that the level of activity had changed.

The budget needs to be restated to show the expectation based on 1,500 units.

The comparison between budget and actual would be as follows:

	Revised budget £	**Actual** £	**Variance** £
Sales	30,000	29,250	750 F
Direct materials	4,500	3,600	900 F
Direct labour	9,000	9,300	300 A
Variable expenses	3,000	2,850	150 F
Fixed costs	5,000	5,100	100 A
Total costs	21,500	20,850	650 F
Profit	8,500	8,400	100 A

This now shows that the profit from 1,500 units should have been £8,500 and was only £8,400, so far from celebrating the actual results, we should be considering why they were £100 less than expected. And we should be investigating the other variances which are now apparent.

Having restated the budget to reflect the actual level of activity, the variances which are now shown are due to efficiency and cost, and not due to the change in the level of activity.

Activity 28

A firm budgets to sell 3,000 units during July, at £25 each. Variable costs are budgeted at £10 for materials, £8 for labour and £2 for expenses, with fixed costs of £5,000. Actual results are sales of 2,500 units for £28 each. Actual costs are materials £26,000, labour £18,000, variable expenses £5,500 and fixed expenses £4,500. Produce a flexible budget which shows the variances.

See Feedback section for answer to this activity.

Summary

Now that you have completed this chapter you should understand the importance of preparing and using budgets for monitoring and control. You should appreciate where the responsibility for budget preparation lies, and be able to prepare a variety of budgets. You should understand the nature and purpose of the flexible budget, and the need to investigate further into the variances that occur.

Review and discussion questions

1 Why do you think budgets are prepared? How often should they be prepared, and how long a period should they cover?
2 Is it necessary to involve people in the preparation of budgets? Can't the accountant do it all?
3 What is meant by the 'principal budget factor'?
4 How many different kinds of budget do you know of?
5 What is the master budget?
6 Once a budget is prepared, it should be adhered to at all costs. Do you agree?
7 If the budget is for 1,000 units and only 800 are produced and sold, then you are bound to have lower revenue, lower costs, and lower profit. Is this right? How can you tell what revenue, costs and profit you should expect for 800 units?

Case study

George has been in business for several years as a manufacturer of waterproof jackets. He buys the basic materials each month, purchasing a fixed quantity because he gets a ten per cent discount that way. The supplier gives him two months' credit. He buys zips, buttons and trimmings from a warehouse whenever it has special offers available – but he has to pay cash at once for those. He has four full-time machinists who work a fixed number of hours per week. Unfortunately, demand is seasonal, and in the summer months his sales are only about one-quarter what they are in the winter. The production is generally easier then, with machinists producing about 30 jackets a week each. If a harsh winter is forecast, he pays his four workers extra to produce more jackets, by getting them to work overtime. Sometimes this extra production causes a shortage of materials, and he has to go to another supplier to get extra stocks – at a higher cost than his normal supplier.

Two of the workers would like to work fewer hours, and are prepared to work from home when extra goods are needed. George also employs a supervisor for the four machinists, who is responsible for keeping an eye on stocks, checking quality and making sure the targets are met. When demand is high, the machinists struggle to complete the work, and quality suffers. The supervisor has complained that the targets then are not achievable, but at other times they are producing more than they sell, and stocks are piling up.

George has never produced any detailed budgets. He just knows that he can sell the jackets for £100 each, and the materials and labour (at basic rate) cost £50. His fixed overheads are fairly low, so he is not worried about the situation. If the two machinists want to reduce their hours, he will employ two other machinists to make up the time.

Advise George on the benefits of preparing budgets, and the types of budgets he could usefully use in his business.

Identify your own role in the preparation and use of one or more budgets in your place of work.

If you are not currently involved in budgeting identify any areas where you could usefully contribute to the budgeting process, or where you could use budgets to monitor and control your own work.

Describe the types of budgets you are/could be involved with, and your contribution to their preparation and use. Explain how the budgets are/could be prepared, what constraints are put upon them, and their use or potential use in the process of monitoring and control. Can you suggest any areas where the budgeting process might be improved?

8 Management accounts

Learning objectives

At the end of this chapter you will be able to:

- explain the purpose of manufacturing accounts
- explain the treatment of work in progress
- demonstrate the preparation of a manufacturing account
- prepare operating statements
- prepare cost statements
- prepare productivity and efficiency statements

Introduction

As discussed in Chapter 2, management accounts aim to provide managers at all levels with the information they need to enable them to plan, control and make decisions. The information provided in management accounts is largely internal and highly detailed. It is also provided at regular intervals throughout the year, perhaps monthly, or even weekly or daily. It is not usually available to 'outsiders' and some of it is even confidential. It is, nevertheless, very important as a tool to enable managers to do their jobs.

Management accounting systems do not provide just monetary information, but might include information on:

- number of hours worked by employees
- quantities produced
- number of outstanding orders
- customers who have not paid
- maintenance records for machinery
- number of machine stoppages due to faulty materials
- customer complaints

and so on. Much of this information would never be disclosed to the public.

Much of management accounting is to do with forward planning and budgeting, but these are often based on historic reports and information. This chapter looks at different types of management accounts.

Manufacturing accounts

Organizations which make their own goods to sell incur different kinds of expenses to those which buy in goods ready-made to sell. Manufacturers need to prepare a *manufacturing account* to bring together all the costs of making goods, which must be differentiated from the costs of selling and delivering goods and providing administrative support.

The manufacturing account collects together the factory or production expenses, in order to arrive at the factory cost of goods completed during the period. This figure is then passed to the trading account to form part of the calculation of gross profit.

Manufacturing costs

Manufacturing costs are those incurred in production, whether direct or indirect. They are sometimes referred to as 'factory costs' and 'production costs'. Direct costs will include direct materials and labour, and sometimes direct expenses. The total of these is called *prime cost*. Indirect costs include expenses such as factory rent and rates, depreciation of factory machinery and factory insurance.

These expenses are often charged in total to the ledger accounts when they are incurred, and a proportion is taken to be a factory cost, with the remainder taken to be an administrative cost.

Manufacturing costs are brought together in the manufacturing account.

Work in progress (WIP)

Many manufacturers start and end the period with stocks of goods which are only partly completed. These are known as work in progress or semi-finished goods. During the period, part of the production costs will be incurred in the completion of the opening WIP, and part will be incurred in producing closing WIP. The production cost incurred during the period will need to be adjusted by adding in the opening WIP and deducted the closing WIP.

Preparing a manufacturing account

Example

Patricia gives you the following extract of balances from her ledgers at 30 June xxx1

	£000	£000
Sales		280
Purchases of raw materials	108	
Opening stock – raw materials	50	
WIP	39	
finished goods	45	
Labour costs – direct	12	
factory supervisors	8	
administrators	4	
Heat and light	12	
Rates	4	
Insurance – buildings	6	
delivery vans	1	
Buildings at cost	400	
Factory plant and machinery at cost	60	
Delivery vans at cost	20	

She gives you the following additional information at 30 June xxx1

(i)   Closing stocks were:

Raw materials	£40,000
Work in progress	£26,000
Finished goods	£53,000

(ii) Heat and light is to be apportioned two-thirds to the factory and one-third to the offices

(iii) Buildings are to be depreciated at 2.5% per annum on cost

(iv) Delivery vans are to be depreciated at 25% per annum on cost

(v) Plant and machinery is to be depreciated at 10% per annum on cost

(vi) Rates, buildings insurance and buildings depreciation are to be apportioned 50% each to the factory and offices

She asks you to produce a manufacturing account, and a trading and profit and loss account for the year ending 30 June xxx1.

Before you start to prepare the accounts, first of all prepare 'workings' for any figures that you cannot just 'pluck out' of the information.

	Total	Factory portion	Office portion
Heat and light	£12,000	$\frac{2}{3}$ = £9,000	$\frac{1}{3}$ = £6,000
Rates	£4,000	50% = £2,000	50% = £2,000
Insurance	£6,000	50% = £3,000	50% = £3,000
Buildings depreciation	2.5% of £400,000 = £10,000	50% = £5,000	50% = £5,000
Plant depreciation	10% × £60,000	£6,000	
Vans depreciation	25% x £20,000		£5,000

Patricia – Manufacturing account for the year ending 30 June xxx1

	£000	£000
Raw materials:		
Opening stocks		50
Purchases		108
		158
less closing stocks		40
Direct materials consumed		118
Direct labour		12
Prime cost		130
Indirect factory expenses:		
Factory supervisors	6	
Heat and light	8	
Rates	2	
Buildings insurance	3	
Buildings depreciation	5	
Plant depreciation	6	
		30
Total factory cost of production		160
Add: opening work in progress	39	
Less: closing work in progress	26	
		13
Factory cost of goods completed		173

MANAGEMENT ACCOUNTS

Patricia – Trading and profit and loss account for the year ending 30 June xxx1

	£000	£000
Sales		280
less cost of goods sold:		
Opening stocks of finished goods	45	
Factory cost of goods completed	173	
	218	
less closing stocks of finished goods	53	
		165
Gross profit		115
Less expenses:		
Administrators' salaries	4	
Heat and light	4	
Rates	2	
Buildings insurance	3	
Buildings depreciation	5	
Delivery vans depreciation	5	
		23
Net profit for the year		92

The balance sheet at 30 June xxx1 will contain three categories of stocks which should be shown as follows:

	£	£
Current assets		
Stocks: – raw materials	40	
– work in progress	26	
– finished goods	53	
	119	

Activity 29

From the following information regarding the year to 30 September xxx1, prepare a manufacturing account, and a trading and profit and loss account:

		£000
Sales		15,700
Opening stocks	– raw materials	6,700
	– work in progress	3,600
	– finished goods	7,100
Purchases	– raw materials	8,000
Closing stocks	– raw materials	4,600
	– work in progress	4,800
	– finished goods	11,600
Office salaries		100
Direct production wages		1,600
Factory supervisors' wages		5,200
Rent of factory		400
Rent of offices		150
Depreciation of production machinery		300
Production power costs		1,300
Heating and lighting costs (40% factory)		250
Depreciation of office machinery		200
Rates (80% factory)		1,000
Delivery costs on sales		120
Delivery costs on purchases		150
General office expenses		180

See Feedback section for answer to this activity.

Cost statements

Any statement which includes the costs of doing something is a cost statement. A cost statement does not include income or profit – only costs.

Some activities which need cost statements do not provide any income or profit anyway – for example the housekeeping unit in a hospital keeps the wards clean and ready for occupation, and incurs costs in doing so, but it does not receive any income.

A cost statement might concern the cost of a hospital operation, the cost of a whole department, or the cost of a special activity, such as an open day in a school.

In this section of the book, the example of a hotel is used to illustrate the various statements and the concepts behind them. Most of you will have used hotels at some time, on business or for holidays, parties, wedding receptions, and so should be able to identify the areas covered.

A cost statement might cover a period in time, say a month or a year; or it might be a 'one-off' - a wedding, perhaps.

It should show what the cost is made up of, and how the total is arrived at.

Examples of cost statements in a hotel, are:

- standard recipes
- labour (wages) costs for a department for a week
- maintenance costs for kitchen equipment for the year
- costs of the housekeeping department for a week
- kitchen production costs for a week
- the cost of a special function

Here is an example of a wages cost statement:

Departmental wages cost statement – Restaurant
Month: December xxx1

Staff category	Basic wages £	Overtime £	Pension £	Total £
Manager	1,500	–	60	1,560
Assistant manager	1,000	–	40	1,040
Waiting staff	3,000	1,000	120	4,120
Total	5,500	1,000	220	6,720

Here is an example of a cost statement for a wedding reception:

Cost statement – Wedding reception, 11 July xxx1

Item	Units	Cost per unit £	Total cost £
3-course dinner, menu B	70	10	700
Sherry on arrival	8 bottles	5	40
Wine – Bordeaux, bin 123	10 bottles	4	40
– Chardonnay, bin 46	10 bottles	5	50
Champagne – bin 12	10 bottles	20	200
Table decorations, place cards	70	1	70
Total			1,100

The total of £1,100 might be used to calculate the charge, by adding a 'mark-up' of, say, sixty per cent, to give a selling price of £1,760. This would cover the cost of the room, staff wages and other overheads.

Investigate 12

Obtain a cost statement from your own organization. What information does it contain?

Activity 30

Produce a cost statement for a college to provide a conference for managers acting as mentors to their employees who are attending one of the college's courses.

There are 40 employers. Conference room hire is £80. Lunch, dinner and general refreshments are £35 per person. The college intends to provide 10 bottles each of red and white wine at £8 per bottle. Stationery and brochures will cost £3 per pack. Hire of overhead projector is £20. Overtime paid to college staff attending the conference is £100 per person, and four staff are expected to attend. Overnight accommodation is £50 per person. Include the staff in your calculation of meals and accommodation.

See Feedback section for answer to this activity.

Operating statements

An operating statement is prepared for particular operations or departments. Some may be 'revenue earning', in which case the operating statement will show the revenue and profit, as well as the costs incurred.

Some operations have no income – the laundry department in a hotel, for example – and therefore, have no profit. In a hospital or a prison, there is no income from sales (although there is income from the government), but they may still produce an operating statement to suit their own needs.

The costs of some departments are spread among others – the cost of the laundry department might be spread between accommodation (rooms) and restaurant, because both of these need to use the services of the laundry department for clean linen.

MANAGEMENT ACCOUNTS

Activity 31

How many departments in a large hotel can you think of which earn revenue? How many can you think of which do not earn revenue?

See Feedback section for answer to this activity.

The operating statement often shows the actual figures and the budgeted figures as well for comparison, and 'year-to-date' figures.

An operating statement only shows those costs which are connected with that department or activity – general costs (such as bank charges, administration, telephone) would not appear on it, unless they can be allocated or apportioned to that department or activity. These general costs are sometimes called 'undistributed costs'.

Only items which have been used up or consumed during the period are included on the operating statement. For example, food and drink costing £6,000 may have been bought, but £2,000 is still unused at the end of the period. Therefore, only £4,000 worth of food and drink is shown as an expense on the operating statement.

Remember that the examples given here are of a restaurant, so we refer to 'food and drink', 'kitchen wages', etc., but if we were dealing with another type of outlet the costs might have different descriptions.

An example of a simple operating statement for a restaurant, for the month of July, might be as follows:

Express Hotels Ltd Restaurant Operating Statement July xxx1

	Actual		Budget		Change
	£	%	£	%	%
Sales	10,000	100	11,000	100.00	–9
Food and drink costs	4,000	40	4,500	40.90	–11
Gross profit	6,000	60	6,500	59.10	–8
Direct wages	2,500	25	2,400	21.80	4
Gross operating profit	3,500	35	4,100	37.30	–14
Restaurant expenses	1,500	15	1,600	14.60	–6
Net operating profit	2,000	20	2,500	22.70	–20
Apportioned expenses	550	5	550	5.00	–
Net margin	1,450	15	1,950	17.70	–26

Note that the operating statement above shows four different levels of profit:

- gross profit
- gross operating profit
- net operating profit
- net margin

This gives rather more detail than the profit and loss accounts that you have looked at earlier in this book.

Gross profit

In a restaurant the most significant cost is usually food. Many restaurants find it useful to calculate the profit after deducting the cost of food and drink. This is known as the gross profit.

Gross profit equals the selling price less the cost of the food and drink.

The restaurant operating statement of Express Hotels Ltd, shows that the actual gross profit for July is £6,000:

Sales	£10,000
less Food and drink costs	£ 4,000
Gross profit	£ 6,000

Gross operating profit

The cost of kitchen and restaurant wages is also a significant cost in the running of the restaurant, so another level of profit can be calculated, after deducting food, drink and direct wages - this is known as gross operating profit.

Gross operating profit equals the sales less the cost of food and drink and direct wages.

The restaurant operating statement for Express Hotels Ltd, shows that the actual gross operating profit for July is £3,500:

Sales		£10,000
less Food and drink costs	£4,000	
less Wages	£2,500	
		£ 6,500
Gross operating profit		£ 3,500

Another way of calculating gross operating profit is gross profit less direct wages. Both methods should give the same answer.

Net operating profit

When other restaurant expenses have been deducted, such as the manager's salary, laundry costs, training, etc., the net operating profit is produced.

Net operating profit is the sales less all other *allocated* expenses of the department for which we are preparing the operating statement.

The operating statement for Express Hotels Ltd shows that the actual net operating profit for July is £2,000:

Sales		£10,000
less Food and drink costs	£4,000	
less Wages	£2,500	
less Restaurant expenses	£1,500	
		£ 8,000
Net operating profit		£ 2,000

Another way of calculating net operating profit is gross operating profit less other expenses. Both methods should give the same answer.

Net margin

This is the final profit after deducting *apportioned expenses*, such as a share of heat and light, rates, insurance, etc.

Additional columns

You will notice in the operating statement that there are also three columns showing percentages. The one under the *Actual* column shows each figure as a percentage of the actual sales. For example, actual direct wages were £2,500 and actual sales were £10,000. So direct wages were 25% of actual sales.

The one under the *Budget* column shows each figure as a percentage of the budgeted sales. Budgeted direct wages were £2,400 and budgeted sales were £11,000. So budgeted direct wages were 21.8% of budgeted sales.

The final column shows the change as a percentage of the budget. Food and drink costs were £500 lower than the budget of £4,500, which is 11%.

Activity 32

Draw up an operating statement for a student refectory for the month of May, and for the year to date, from the following information:

Sales	– May £18,000
	– January–April £60,000
Food costs	– May £8,100
	– January–April £27,780
Wages	– May £3,600
	– January–April £13,560
Other expenses	– May £2,700
	– January–April £9,780

See Feedback section for answer to this activity.

Combined operating statements

Where an organization has different operating departments or activities, these can be shown together on a single statement. There are many different layouts – the example here is only a suggestion, using Express Hotels Ltd, with three departments of Rooms, Restaurant and Bar.

Express Hotels Ltd Operating Statement July xxx1

	Rooms £	Restaurant £	Bar £	Total £
Sales	30,000	10,000	2,500	42,500
Direct materials	–	4,000	1,200	5,200
Gross operating profit	30,000	6,000	1,300	37,300
Direct wages	6,000	2,500	800	9,300
Gross profit	24,000	3,500	500	28,000
Allocated expenses	600	1,500	100	2,200
Net operating profit	23,400	2,000	400	25,800
Apportioned expenses	2,000	550	100	2,650
Net margin	21,400	1,450	300	23,150
Less undistributed expenses:				
Finance charges			4,300	
Reception costs			11,000	
				15,300
Net profit				7,850

Productivity and efficiency statements

Not all management reports are to do with monetary values. Many are based on quantities or other measures of activity. A statement of machine usage is called a machine utilization statement.

A firm has four machines. Each is capable of producing 200 units a week. During Week 45, the production was recorded, and reasons for 'downtime' (lack of productivity) were identified. The machine utilization statement for Week 45, might be as follows:

Machine	A		B		C		D	
	Hours	%	Hours	%	Hours	%	Hours	%
Maximum usage	200	100	200	100	200	100	200	100
Actual usage	100	50	160	80	140	70	180	90
Breakdown time	40	20	20	10	20	10	20	10
Changeover time	60	30	20	10	40	20		

Produce a vehicle utilization statement for Week 17, from the following data:

Vehicles are budgeted to travel for 40 hours per week each. Actual time recorded was as follows:

Vehicle A – travel time 30 hours, breakdown 5 hours, idle time 5 hours
Vehicle B – travel time 30 hours, idle time 10 hours
Vehicle C – travel time 35 hours, idle time 5 hours
Vehicle C – travel time 40 hours

See Feedback section for answer to this activity.

Summary

Now that you have completed this chapter you should understand the purpose of manufacturing accounts, and the different types of costs contained within them. You should be able to distinguish between costs which are connected with manufacturing, as opposed to those connected with trading or administration. You should be able to prepare a manufacturing account with appropriate sub-headings and adjustment for work in progress. You should be able to prepare various kinds of cost, operating statement and productivity statements for different situations.

Review and discussion questions

1 Identify the types of information that management accounts might provide.
2 What are the main headings in a manufacturing account?
3 What is prime cost?
4 Give five examples of cost statements in an airline company.
5 What is the difference between a cost statement and an operating statement?
6 What is a productivity/efficiency statement? How useful is it to management.

Case study

Professional and Personal Performance (PPP) is an organization which provides consultancy services to small businesses that wish to improve on their image and professional approach in the business world. There are ten trainers employed by the firm, to give one-to-one advice, run courses for groups of people at PPP's premises, and give in-house courses to larger organizations. PPP develops its own training materials, using its own printing and desk-top publishing facilities, staffed by a team of four people. PPP also sells textbooks and training materials.

Devise a selection of management reports which would assist in the control of costs, productivity and efficiency for the organization.

Work-based assignment

Collect a sample of the various management reports produced by your organization for internal use. Identify any in which you are personally involved and comment on how they are prepared. What use is made of such reports to monitor and control activities and to enhance performance?

9 Costing methods

Learning objectives

At the end of this chapter you will be able to:

- understand the differences between different costing methods
- understand the principles of *absorption costing*
- understand the principles of *marginal costing*
- apply the concept of *contribution*
- calculate and appreciate the importance of the break-even point
- understand the concept and use of standard costing methods
- appreciate the usefulness of activity-based costing
- calculate the cost of a product or service using a variety of costing methods
- make simple decisions using different costing methods

Introduction

This chapter looks at different methods of calculating costs. Each method is based on different assumptions, but all methods consider the fact that prices have to be quoted for orders before the actual costs of the job or project are known.

There are four main costing systems. These are:

- absorption costing
- marginal costing
- standard costing
- activity-based costing

There is no single 'best' method of calculating costs. Each has its own advantages and disadvantages and is more appropriate than the others in particular circumstances.

Absorption costing

This is based on the assumption that the cost of a unit should include not only the direct costs associated with that unit, but also a proportion of the overheads incurred. Direct costs will have been allocated directly to the production cost centre/cost units concerned; indirect costs (overheads) will by now have been apportioned in various ways to the same cost centres.

Example

A product takes £5 in direct materials, £4 in direct labour, £3 in variable overheads, and £6 as a proportion of the indirect costs. The total cost of a product is, therefore, £18.

Example

A product is produced in batches of 1,000. Materials cost £5,000, labour costs £4,000, variable overheads cost £3,000 and fixed costs are £6,000.

The cost of a single unit can be calculated as follows:

	£
Materials costs	5,000
Labour costs	4,000
Variable overhead costs	3,000
Fixed costs	6,000
Total costs	18,000

Divided by 1,000 units = £18 per unit

Absorption costing in principle

Absorption costing has an effect on the profits of the business.

In the above example, the cost of a unit is calculated as £18.

Supposing that of the 1,000 units produced, only 600 are sold, for £20 each.

The profit might be calculated as follows:

Sales	600 × £20	£12,000
Cost of sales		
	600 × £18	£10,800
Gross profit		£ 1,200

In addition, there would be closing stock of 400 units valued at £18 each = £7,200.

Absorption costing and the effect on profits

Fixed costs are often costs which cannot be avoided, such as rent and rates, and which have to be paid whatever the level of activity. Suppose that the fixed costs above were unavoidable and had to be paid in the current year, irrespective of the level of activity or sales.

We might still sell 600 units at £20 each, and incur direct costs as before, i.e. £12,000 (materials £5,000, labour £4,000, variable overheads £3,000) for 1,000 units. This amounts to £12 per unit.

The profit could be calculated as follows:

Sales	600 × £20	£12,000
Cost of sales		
	600 × £12	£ 7,200
		£ 4,800
Less fixed costs		£ 6,000
Loss		£ 1,200

The stock unsold would be valued at 400 × £12 each = £4,800.

Which result is the correct one?

Well, from an accounting point of view, the latter is correct because it takes account of the fact that fixed costs are nothing to do with the production or sales, but are to do with the period concerned. Rent and rates, for example, have to be paid irrespective of the level of production or sales, and so have no connection with the level of activity.

But if you are trying to determine a selling price, you cannot ignore the fixed costs.

The biggest problem is in determining the budgeted level of activity. If we could guarantee to sell all the production of 1,000 units, then the whole of the fixed costs could be absorbed, and a profit would be made whichever method of calculation was used.

Absorption costing is usually used to determine a selling price which will cover all the costs incurred. In the above example, if variable costs amount to £12 per unit, and overheads are absorbed at £6 per unit, it is assumed that the selling price must be at least £18 per unit in order to make any profit. If the selling price is £20 a unit then the profit will be £1,200.

Activity 34

An advertising consultancy prices its jobs on the expected number of executive hours. It therefore apportions its overheads on the same basis. Overheads for next month are budgeted at £10,000 and the total expected executive hours amount to 400. A particular job is expected to take 20 hours. The job will also incur direct material costs of £350, and executive hours are costed at £45 per hour.

Calculate the selling price necessary to make a profit of £600.

See Feedback section for answer to this activity.

Marginal costing

This is based on the assumption that the cost of a unit should include only the additional or incremental cost of producing that unit. In effect, this means that the marginal cost includes only variable costs as these are the only ones which are an additional cost. In making decisions, such as whether to make extra units, fixed costs should be ignored as they are not affected.

Marginal costing relies on each unit sold making a contribution to the organization.

Contribution is the difference between selling price and marginal cost. It is the amount which is available to go towards the fixed costs, or, if these have already been covered by previous sales, it goes towards profit.

Contribution = Sales − Variable costs

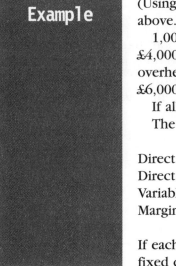

Example

(Using the same figures as in the absorption costing example above.)

1,000 units of a product take £5,000 of direct materials, £4,000 of direct labour per year and £3,000 of variable overheads. Each unit sells for £20, and fixed costs amount to £6,000 per year.

If all units are sold, the profit is £2,000

The variable or marginal cost of a unit is £12:

Direct material	£ 5 per unit	(£5,000/1,000 units)
Direct labour	£ 4 per unit	(£4,000/1,000 units)
Variable overheads	£ 3 per unit	(£3,000/1,000 units)
Marginal cost	£12 per unit	

If each unit sells for £20, then it contributes £8 towards the fixed costs.

The importance of 'contribution'

Contribution is a very important concept in management accounting. An item contributes if its selling price exceeds its variable or marginal cost.

If we assume that fixed costs are to be paid irrespective of production, then any contribution towards them is welcome.

Imagine you own your own house, and the fixed outgoings (mortgage, insurance, etc.) are £500 per month. Someone offers to share your house and pays £50 per week. You estimate that her food and additional electricity, etc. will take up £30 of that. That means you have £20 to contribute towards your mortgage each week. Not a lot, but better than nothing. You would prefer to have a lodger who pays £70 per week, but you can't find one.

That is the principle of 'contribution'. Any contribution, however small, is worth having from an accounting point of view.

In the example above, each unit contributed £8 towards the fixed costs.

If only 600 units are sold, this brings in a contribution of £4,800 which is not enough to cover the fixed costs – but it is better than nothing. If all 1,000 units are sold the contribution will be £8,000, which covers the fixed costs and produces £2,000 of profit.

Contribution − Fixed costs = Profit

Marginal costing and decision making

If we use aborption costing to determine our selling price, we will hopefully cover all our costs, both fixed and variable. In the example above, if we sell 1,000 units for £20 we will cover our fixed costs and make a profit.

In fact, the absorption cost of a unit tells us that we can sell it for less than £20 and still make a profit:

Total cost of 1,000 units   £18,000
Selling price needed to cover total costs = £18 per unit

You might think that £18 is the minimum we should charge for a unit. But suppose that our customers are only prepared to pay £15 per unit. Do we turn them away? If we turn them away, we will still have to pay our fixed costs of £6,000. So we will make a loss of £3,000.

If we sell them at £16 each, with variable costs of £12 each, we will obtain contribution of £4 per unit, i.e. £4,000 in total – so then our loss will only be £2,000. Which would you prefer? A loss of £3,000 or a loss of £2,000.

This illustrates that contribution is always useful, even if it is not sufficient to cover the fixed costs.

Consider the following case:

Variable costs per unit   £10
Fixed costs per annum   £12,000

How much should you charge per unit?

A difficult question. It might depend on how many you expect to sell.

If you expect to sell 1,000 then the variable cost of £10 will be increased by the fixed cost of £12 each = £22 per unit.

Suppose you only expect to sell 100 units? The variable cost is still £10, but the fixed cost would be £120. Could you sell a unit for £130? If so, great, get on with it. But if the going rate for a unit is only, say £30, what should you do?

Well, you could say no to offers of only £30. You would end up with no sales, and still have to pay the fixed costs of £12,000.

But if you said 'yes' to offers of £30, each one would contribute £20 towards your fixed costs.

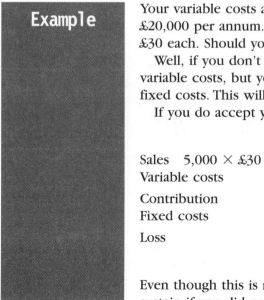

Example

Your variable costs are £20 per unit, and fixed costs are £20,000 per annum. You receive an order for 5,000 units at £30 each. Should you accept?

Well, if you don't accept, you will have no sales, and no variable costs, but you will still have to pay out the £20,000 in fixed costs. This will be your loss.

If you do accept you will have the following situation:

Sales 5,000 × £30	£15,000
Variable costs	£10,000
Contribution	£ 5,000
Fixed costs	£20,000
Loss	£15,000

Even though this is not ideal, the loss is less than you would sustain if you did not accept the order.

COSTING METHODS

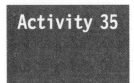

Activity 35

A new customer offers to buy 100 units for £20 each. Normal selling price is £30. The absorption cost of a unit is £26, but the marginal cost is only £18. Should the offer be accepted?

See Feedback section for answer to this activity.

Example

Using the same figures again, suppose only 800 units have been sold to date at the full price of £30. The contribution received so far would be 800 × £12 per unit, i.e. £9,600. This falls short of the £12,000 fixed costs by £2,400. The organization needs to make a further £2,400 contribution or it is in trouble.

Suppose a customer offers to buy 500 units at £22. Should you accept?

Yes. This price makes a contribution of £4 per unit, so £2,000 extra contribution will result from this decision. This is still not quite enough to cover all the fixed costs – but we're nearly there. So the order is worth having.

Activity 36

Calculate the profit, showing the amount of contribution clearly, from the following information regarding 5,000 products made and sold during March:

Direct materials cost	£25,000
Direct labour cost	£20,000
Fixed costs	£15,000
Selling price	£15 per unit

Calculate the extra profit to be made if an additional 20 units are sold at the same selling price.

If an order is received for an additional 500 units at a selling price of only £10 each, should this be accepted?

See Feedback section for answer to this activity.

Marginal costing and the break-even point

The break-even point is the point at which no profit (and no loss) is made. Using marginal costing terminology, it is the point at which the contribution from products exactly equals the fixed costs to be covered.

RESOURCES MANAGEMENT

Example

In our earlier example, the contribution of a unit was found as follows:

Selling price	£30
Variable cost	£18
Contribution per unit	£12

The fixed costs for the year were £12,000, so the firm needed to sell enough units contributing £12 each to raise £12,000 in order to break even. The break-even point therefore is 1,000 units, i.e.

Fixed costs/contribution per unit = £12,000/£12 = 1,000 units

Each unit up to 1,000 contributes towards the fixed costs. Once the break-even point has been reached, then each additional unit contributes entirely to profit.

Activity 37

Calculate the break-even point from the following information regarding 5,000 products made and sold during March:

Direct materials costs	£25,000
Direct labour cost	£20,000
Fixed costs	£15,000
Selling price	£15 per unit

See Feedback section for answer to this activity.

Standard costing

Absorption costing is best suited to making decisions about general selling prices. Marginal costing is best suited to making decisions about one-off orders or short runs.

Many manufacturers make things in bulk throughout the year. Materials, labour and overhead costs are constantly changing, but customers really need a constant selling price. Standard costing is a technique which assists in this.

A standard cost is set at the beginning of the year which takes into account the *expected* cost of materials, labour and overheads for the whole year, including anticipated price rises. The setting of standard costs needs to be very

COSTING METHODS

carefully undertaken. It involves careful measurement of the following:

- the quantity of material used in each product
- the cost of material per kg, ton, metre, etc.
- the labour hours taken for each product
- the hourly rate of labour
- the basis of overheads incurred for each product e.g. the number of machine hours
- the cost of variable overheads per machine hour
- the fixed costs

It also requires careful estimate of the expected level of activity.

The estimates must assume that there is access to good quality materials, efficient labour and that there are clearly defined working methods. Once the standards have been set, they set the scene for the next twelve months, so it is important that they are as accurate as possible.

When the actual figures are known, they are compared to the standards used, and any differences (variances) are investigated.

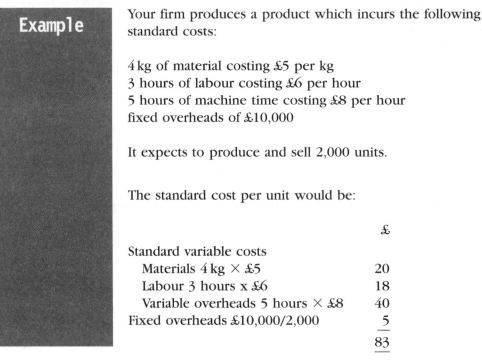

Example

Your firm produces a product which incurs the following standard costs:

4 kg of material costing £5 per kg
3 hours of labour costing £6 per hour
5 hours of machine time costing £8 per hour
fixed overheads of £10,000

It expects to produce and sell 2,000 units.

The standard cost per unit would be:

	£
Standard variable costs	
Materials 4 kg × £5	20
Labour 3 hours x £6	18
Variable overheads 5 hours × £8	40
Fixed overheads £10,000/2,000	5
	83

Suppose that during the last year, 2,500 units were produced and sold, and the costs were:

Materials	£49,500
Labour	£48,000
Variable overheads	£90,000
Fixed overheads	£ 6,000

You might remember from your study of Chapter 7, that actual results should be compared with a *flexible* budget, rather than a fixed one. So, the actual materials cost of £49,500 should be compared with the standard materials cost of 2,500 units, which is:

$$2,500 \times £20 = £50,000$$

So, actual materials cost £500 less than the standard cost for 2,500 units. Isn't that good?

Not necessarily. You need to break down the actual cost into the amount of material used and the price paid for it, and compare it with the standard amount of material used and the expected price.

Suppose that the actual material used was 9,000 kg at £5.50 per kg (£49,500 in total).

We have two variances here – the amount of material used is different from that standard, and the price of the material is different too.

The total variance of £500 is due to the two variances.

The variance due to materials *usage* is calculated as:

2,500 units should have used 10,000 kg of material at £5 per kg	= £50,000
Actual usage of 9,000 kg at a standard cost of £5 per kg	= £45,000
Thus there is a favourable materials usage variance of	£5,000

The variance due to materials *price* is calculated as:

Usage of 9,000 kg of materials should have cost £5 per kg	= £45,000
Actual cost of 9,000 kg of materials was	= £49,500
Thus there is an unfavourable materials price variance of	£4,500

Total materials variance £500 Favourable

Activity 38

The standard cost of one barrel of cutting fluid has been set as follows:

	£
Direct labour, 3 hours @ £4 per hour	12
Direct materials, 6 kg @ £8 per kg	48
Variable overheads	10
	70

Fixed overheads are budgeted at £18,000 per month, for standard output of 2,000 barrels, with a selling price of £100 per barrel.

Actual output in Month 8 was 2,300 barrels, sold for £253,000. Actual costs were as follows:

	£
Direct labour, 2 hours @ £5 per hour	10
Direct materials, 8 kg @ £7 per kg	56
Variable overheads	12
	78

Fixed overheads were £19,000.

Produce a flexible budget for the month, and analyse the materials variances which have occurred.

See Feedback section for answer to this activity.

Activity-based costing (ABC)

Activity-based costing is a method which attempts to be much more precise than those previously mentioned. It is based on the assumption that it is *activities* which cause costs to be incurred, and not quantities or hours spent.

As a simple example, suppose that an organization makes two products, A and B. A takes 10 hours of labour, and B takes 5 hours, costing £4 per hour. Both take the same amount of material (£10), and 1,000 each are produced each year.

Suppose that factory overheads include set-up costs, supervisor's salary and purchase ordering costs. They are £30,000 for the year.

How could this be apportioned between the two products?

Apportioning overheads by quantity produced

Well, it could be apportioned equally, as they both have the same quantities, i.e. 1,000 each, which is £15.00 per unit. The costs of each would then be:

	A	B
Materials	10.00	10.00
Labour	40.00	20.00
Overheads	15.00	15.00
Total cost	65.00	45.00

Appportioning overheads by hours taken to produce

Overheads could be apportioned on the number of labour hours, with A taking twice as much as B. That would mean £20,000 for A (£20 a unit), and £10,000 for B (£10 a unit). The costs would then be:

	A	B
Materials	10.00	10.00
Labour	40.00	20.00
Overheads	20.00	10.00
Total cost	70.00	40.00

This makes B even cheaper.

Apportioning overheads on the basis of activities carried out

Suppose that A is made in batches of 250 at a time. B is made in batches of 50 at a time. So A has four production runs a year, while B has twenty.

Every time there is a new production run, the machinery needs to be reset. The supervisor has to be involved in this. It takes the same amount of time to set up both products. Every production run also involves ordering materials. It takes the same time to order the £2,500 worth of materials for A as it does to order the £500 worth of materials for B – one phone call, one purchase order, one goods received note, etc.

So the £30,000 worth of factory overheads is incurred because of the change in production runs. A has four runs, B has twenty runs.

The overheads could be apportioned on the basis of production runs. That would be as follows:

- Each production run costs £1,250 (£30,000 divided by 24 runs)
- Product A has 4 runs, so overheads would be £5,000 (4 runs × £1,250 per run). Each unit, therefore, takes up £5 (£5,000 divided by 1,000 units).
- Product B has 20 runs, so overheads would be £25,000 (20 runs × £1,250 per run). Each unit, therefore, takes up £25 (£25,000 divided by 1,000 units)

The costs of the two products looks very different now:

	A	B
Materials	10.00	10.00
Labour	40.00	20.00
Overheads	5.00	25.00
Total cost	55.00	55.00

Using this method, both products cost the same.

Cost drivers

The *activity* which causes the cost to be incurred, is called a *cost driver*. In the above example, it is production runs which are the cost driver. Each run costs £1,250. So it seems sensible to say that a product which has more runs should be apportioned more of the overheads.

The above example was made very simple by making the assumption that each run took the same amount of set-up time, supervision, and purchasing costs. In the real world, things would be much more complicated. There might be many cost drivers for a single product. Examples include:

- purchasing
- receipt of materials to store
- set-up of machinery
- supervision
- transfer of materials from store

Cost pools

Each of the activities which drives costs is a *cost pool*. The costs of carrying out the activities are gathered together in the pool. For example, the cost of purchasing might include the wages of the purchasing department staff, equipment used by them, telephone costs, paperwork costs, and of course the overheads apportioned to the purchasing department such as heat and light, insurance, training, etc.

Once the costs have been collected in the pool, then the number of purchases made can be divided into the total cost, to find the cost of each activity.

Example

The total costs of the purchasing department are budgeted at £50,000 per year. The cost pool is therefore £50,000. The number of purchases expected to be made is 10,000 per year. So each purchase costs £5.

A product making one purchase a year is apportioned £5 for purchasing. A product making ten purchases a year is apportioned £50.

Summary

Now that you have completed this chapter you should appreciate that there are several different methods of determining the cost of a product or group of products. You should appreciate the difference between absorption and marginal costing and know when the application of each is most appropriate. You should understand the usefulness of standard costing, in particular to the calculation of variances and the need for investigation into variances. You should appreciate the refinement of activity-based costing and its level of precision.

Review and discussion questions

1 What do you understand by the term 'absorption costing'?
2 What is meant by 'contribution'?
3 Any contribution, however small, is worth having. Do you agree with this statement?
4 Would you sell a product for less than its total cost? Why?
5 What is the break-even point? Why is it important? How is it calculated?
6 What is meant by 'standard costing'?
7 What is meant by activity-based costing?
8 What is a cost pool? What is a cost driver?

COSTING METHODS

Case study

Diana is the production supervisor for a small team of machine operatives. The team is constantly being told that they are not profitable enough. Arguments that are levied against them include the following:

- The fixed costs are high, so high output is needed to cover them.
- Some product lines are unprofitable because they do not cover their fixed costs, and are in danger of being cut from production.
- Selling prices are already too high, so Diana must reduce fixed costs to enable selling prices to be cut.
- An order for 10 extra units had to be refused because it did not cover its total cost, including fixed costs.
- Diana's team produces products with a selling price of £50 and variable costs of £30. Fixed costs apportioned to Diana's team are £10,000. They produce 400 units a month. The team is accused of not covering its costs.
- The standard cost of a product is £30, consisting of materials of £20 and labour of £10. Last month 400 units were produced with a total materials cost of £8,700, and total labour costs of £3,500. Diana was criticized for exceeding her budget of £12,000.

Draft a report to Diana's manager in support of her argument that some, if not all, of the above accusations are unfounded. Include relevant figures to support your case.

Work-based assignment

B1.1
B1.2

Identify the costing methods in use at your workplace. Consider their relevance and appropriateness in particular situations. Produce a list of selling prices or costing statements which have arisen recently and give details of how the figures were arrived at. Were they based on marginal, absorption, activity-based or standard costing methods? Were they based on none of these? Which method would have been most appropriate in your opinion?

10 Purchasing of goods and services

Learning objectives

On completion of this chapter you will be able to:

- explain why careful purchasing of goods and services is important
- describe different methods of purchasing to meet different requirements
- describe the documentation used in the purchasing process

Introduction

It is important that supplies of goods and services are available of the right quality, at the right time, and for the best possible price. If goods and services are incorrect, or worse unavailable, this might prevent an organization from earning its income. Goods and services which cost more than they need to will reduce profits. This chapter looks at good practice in ensuring that organizations obtain goods and services to best fulfil their needs.

Getting the right quality

Whatever is being purchased, the needs of the organization should be carefully considered. The items required should be clearly *specified*. This means that the person requiring the items should draw up a detailed description of what is required. Suppose a hospital needs tinned potatoes. To issue a request merely for tinned potatoes is far too vague. What size of tin is needed? How large should the potatoes be? What grade of potato is required? Are they to be in brine or unsalted? A *purchase specification* is an important part of ensuring the correct quality is obtained.

You would not go into an electrical store and ask for 'a washing machine', and expect to get exactly what you need.

144

You would look for specific features such as spin speed, number of programmes, special treatments, temperature controls, and so on.

Stocks

The types of materials which organizations need varies widely. In a manufacturing or trading organization, the biggest need is for raw materials or goods ready for sale. In other organizations, there are different requirements. For example, a hospital needs to purchase drugs, dressings, food and disinfectants. A grocer needs to purchase fresh, tinned and packaged foods. A stationer buys books, magazines, newspapers and general stationery. A local authority buys building materials, salt and grit for icy roads, dustbin bags, etc. A school buys textbooks, writing materials, pens and crayons.

Consumables

Most organizations require items of stationery for letters, invoices and other documentation. Cleaning materials, toilet supplies, staff canteen supplies are other examples.

Services

Few organizations provide everything for themselves. Many need to 'contract' from others for specialist areas, such as financial advice, advertising, recruitment, training, legal services. Many of these are only required intermittently, rather than on a regular basis.

Overheads

This category covers the day-to-day services such as heat and light, telephone, cleaning, etc. While organizations tend to be less specific when buying these items, there is still a need to determine the quality of the provision.

Fixed assets

The acquisition of fixed assets has its own special problems to consider. Any investment in fixed assets is going to affect an

RESOURCES MANAGEMENT

organization for a long period of time, and therefore mistakes have to be lived with well into the future. Less expensive fixed assets might be purchased in the same way as stocks, from the same kinds of supplier. Larger, more costly fixed assets might involve negotiations with manufacturers to design and build a one-off item, such as a piece of heavy plant, or a building. There might be a need to involve surveyors, architects, solicitors and accountants, as well as those providing the asset.

The timing of supplies

All goods and services should be available when they are required. Delays can result in lost profit and irate staff and customers. Shortages of stocks, consumables, etc. all cause problems which can be time consuming and costly to rectify. Prevention is better than cure.

Adequate control over items already in stock is essential to ensure the smooth running of the organization. Records should be kept of what is in stock, and regular checks should be performed to check the accuracy of the records and to prompt the ordering of new supplies.

Many organizations nowadays make use of computer technology to keep stocks as low as possible and to re-order only when it is essential. This system is known as 'just in time' or JIT.

Re-order levels and quantities

Many organizations record a 're-order level' on their stock records, which tells the storekeeper to order when the level falls to that quantity.

They may also add a 're-order quantity', which determines how much should be ordered at any one time.

The re-order level and quantity need careful determination. They depend on a number of factors:

- past usage
- future usage
- delivery times (also called the 'lead time')
- discounts available for bulk purchases
- payment requirements

For example, if the lead time is several weeks, then the re-order level will be higher than for items with a shorter lead time, to avoid the possibility of a shortage. If there are discounts available for bulk purchase, a larger quantity might be ordered – though this needs to be balanced out against the cost of additional storage space and the need to pay out a larger sum of money.

The re-order level and quantity should be regularly reviewed.

Excess stock

Holding excess stock is expensive. It has to be paid for, which affects cash flow. It needs storage space, perhaps in special conditions, it is more time consuming to keep track of, it might deteriorate or go out of fashion, and it will need insuring.

Choosing a supplier

There are many things to look for when choosing a supplier. Often organizations stick to the same supplier year in, year out, because it is convenient to do so. But they may not be getting the best deal. Obviously, you will choose a supplier who provides the right quality of goods, at the right time and at the best price. But there are a number of other considerations to take into account, such as:

1 The range of products offered. If you can purchase several items from the same supplier you could reduce ordering time, delivery costs and obtain discounts.
2 The reputation of the supplier. Well-established suppliers have a reputation, but some newer suppliers might give better service if you are prepared to take the risk.
3 The quantity of goods required. Some suppliers provide only large quantities and are not suitable for the smaller business, and vice versa of course.
4 Price and payment terms. Some suppliers charge higher prices, but offer greater discounts for prompt payment. Some charge a fee if invoices are not paid on time.
5 Location of the supplier. If you need to view the goods, you might not be prepared to travel far. If you require after-sales service, a distant supplier might be less accessible.

6 Delivery arrangements. Goods might be delivered free of charge, or at a cost. There might be no delivery service at all.

7 Advice and expertise. If you are not an expert yourself, you might need to rely on the advice of the supplier.

8 After-sales service, including guarantees, service and repair agreements, etc.

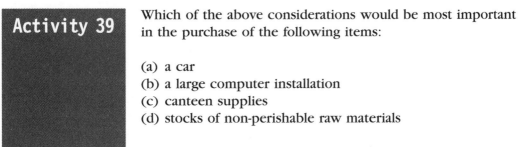

Which of the above considerations would be most important in the purchase of the following items:

(a) a car
(b) a large computer installation
(c) canteen supplies
(d) stocks of non-perishable raw materials

See Feedback section for answer to this activity.

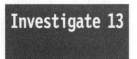

Choose three items which your organization has purchased recently. How was the supplier chosen? What factors were taken into account? Do you feel that the choice was carefully made?

Methods of purchasing

There are several different methods of purchasing. Which method is best for your organization depends on a number of factors:

- how often you need the items (e.g. daily, monthly, as required)
- the quantity you require
- the price you want to pay
- the location of the supplier

The ones we are going to look at are:

- contract purchasing/purchasing by tender
- centralized purchasing

- daily market list or quotation purchasing
- wholesale and cash and carry purchasing
- retail purchasing

We will look at some of these purchasing methods now. It is important to realize that the organization can use several of these methods at one time, and can even use two methods for the same product – for example, contract purchasing can also be centralized.

Contract purchasing/purchasing by tender

A contract is an agreement to do something. Contract purchasing is where the organization contracts to purchase certain supplies from a particular supplier, either for a fixed amount of time or for a fixed quantity of goods.

As a contract is legally binding, great care must be taken to choose the correct one.

A contract for a fixed period of time is suitable for goods which do not vary much in price, otherwise the organization could lose out on price reductions during the period of the contract. A contract for a fixed quantity is suitable for goods which do not deteriorate, and where quantities can be estimated well in advance.

Contract purchasing is usually used by larger organizations who are buying in large enough quantities to strike a good bargain with the supplier. The organization also needs to be able to judge well in advance what quantities it is going to need, otherwise it could over order and be left with goods which it cannot use.

Purchasing by tender is very similar to contract purchasing, except that instead of the organization seeking out different suppliers, it invites the suppliers to contact them to offer prices for the goods it requires. A contract is then probably made with the supplier with the lowest price.

The advantages to an organization of contract purchasing are:

- Continuity of supply is assured. The supplier agrees to supply for some time, and the organization can rely on that regular supply.
- The price is known in advance, making planning much easier, and there are often discounts available for large quantities.

- Time is saved. Once the contract is made, the organization need spend no more time searching for supplies.
- Regular deliveries means that the organization does not need to hold high levels of stock.
- Payments can usually be spread over the time of the contract, perhaps at a fixed amount per month.

The disadvantages of contract purchasing are:

- The choice of suppliers who offer this type of purchasing is limited. This in turn limits the choice of goods which can be bought this way.
- Once the contract is made, the organization cannot take advantage of future price reductions or special offers.
- If the contract is for a fixed quantity, which turns out to be overestimated, overstocking and deterioration could be a problem.
- If the service given by the supplier proves to be unsatisfactory, it can be difficult to break the contract or to find alternative suppliers.

| Activity 40 | Can you think of four types of goods and services which a restaurant might buy using contract purchasing? |

See Feedback section for answer to this activity.

Centralized purchasing

Centralized purchasing is a method of purchasing whereby goods are ordered from a single place (e.g. head office) and then distributed to other parts of the organization.

This method is used by organizations who have several branches, departments or outlets, even perhaps spread across the country. The goods are ordered by a central buying department on behalf of all the branches. The goods may also be delivered to a central warehouse and then delivered to the individual branches on request. Centralized purchasing could easily be combined with contract purchasing for larger organizations.

The advantages of centralized purchasing are:

- The organization can buy in large quantities. Bulk buying means that good discounts can be obtained.

PURCHASING OF GOODS AND SERVICES

- Having a central store means that a wider range of goods is available to the branches, with less chance of running out of stock.
- The central store can be more easily controlled and kept secure, thus reducing the chances of loss or theft.
- Individual branches do not have to keep high stocks of goods, thus the overall stock held by the organization is much lower.
- The quantities being purchased may give the organization the opportunity to insist on special treatment, on delivery for example, or to insist on a certain quality of goods.
- All branches will be using the same types of goods, therefore quality and style will be consistent throughout the organization. A McDonald's cheeseburger is the same in all McDonald's restaurants throughout the country – you can rely on it!
- The person responsible for purchasing becomes an expert at dealing with a range of goods to be purchased.

The disadvantages of centralized purchasing are:

- Individual branches have less control over the choice of supplier and type of goods supplied.
- Loss of freedom of choice to individual branches may mean that branches with particular needs may be unable to meet those needs; similarly, branches with a special flair for a particular service may be unable to provide it.
- Local price reductions or special promotions cannot be utilized.
- There may be delivery problems unless there is an efficient system of distribution of goods from the central warehouse.

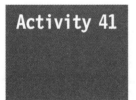

Activity 41

Look around your own town – can you see any organizations which are part of a large chain or group, and which might use centralized purchasing? Which goods might it buy using this method?

See Feedback section for answer to this activity.

Daily market list or quotation purchasing

Purchasing by daily market list or quotation involves obtaining the latest price each day from a number of suppliers, for the goods required.

This method is used for items where the price changes daily or very frequently, such as fresh fruit and vegetables which are often bought from wholesale markets several times a week to make sure of a continuous supply of fresh produce. Each day, several suppliers are contacted to provide quotations for the goods required. This can be done via the telephone, the fax, or, nowadays, using electronic mail, electronic data interchange and the Internet.

The advantages of purchasing by daily market list or quotation are:

- The best price available can be chosen.
- Suppliers compete with each other, thus prices are kept lower.
- Daily purchasing means that supplies can be bought as they are required, and need not take up storage space unnecessarily.
- Fresh produce is available at all times.

The disadvantages of purchasing by daily market list or quotation are:

- It can be time consuming to obtain prices and make choices so frequently.
- Small organizations who purchase in low quantities may not be able to obtain good prices or discounts.
- There is a possibility that goods could be unavailable on a particular day, which could result in shortages for the organization.

Wholesale and cash and carry purchasing

Wholesalers buy from the manufacturer and sell to the other businesses or to retailers.

Cash and carry purchasing is a method of purchasing from depots or warehouses, whereby immediate payment is made for the goods, which must be transported away from the depot by the buyer.

Wholesalers and cash and carry depots often supply goods only in bulk packs. The term 'cash' used to mean that only notes and coins were accepted as payment, but nowadays cheques and credit cards are accepted as well. However, they still insist that purchases are paid for at once by one of these methods.

Cash and carries are usually fairly local – most medium-sized towns have one. Some are very specialized, selling only sweets and tobacco for example, or selling Chinese foods. Others are more general, selling a wider range of goods.

Some wholesalers operate on a 'mail-order' basis by issuing catalogues to their customers.

The advantages of wholesale and cash and carry purchasing are:

- Prices are lower, due to bulk packaging and purchasing, customers serving themselves, poor surroundings.
- There are no minimum order levels, except for the bulk packs, so customers need not buy in very large quantities.
- Although delivery is the customer's responsibility, most are fairly local so delivery costs are not too high.
- Being local means that customers have access to fresh supplies regularly and overstocking can be avoided.
- The range and quality of products can be viewed before purchase.

The disadvantages of wholesale and cash and carry purchasing are:

- There may be no delivery service (except for mail-order purchasing).
- Credit is not available.
- Some products may be out of stock at times of shortages, thus there is no guarantee of availability.

Retail purchasing

Retail purchasing is purchasing from outlets which supply the public.

This is useful for items which are needed at short notice, perhaps because the normal delivery has not arrived, or because absolute freshness is required. The advantage is the ease of purchasing by this method, but the disadvantage is that the price may be higher than other methods.

| **Activity 42** |

Consider the table below showing a variety of products required by different types of caterer. Complete the table with the most appropriate method of purchasing for each.

	Small hotel with restaurant	Large hospital	Mobile take-away	Large international hotel
Fresh parsley for garnishing dishes				
Fresh chicken portions				
Frozen beefburger				
Liquid disinfectant				
Serviettes				
Potatoes				

See Feedback section for answer to this activity.

The stages in the purchasing process

The stages in the purchasing process are:

1 initial requisition
2 purchase specification
3 quotation
4 purchase order
5 receipt of goods (and return of unwanted items)
6 invoicing
7 payment

Initial requistion

All goods required by an organization should be requested on this document. It is raised by the person who needs to use the goods. This might be the production department, the storekeeper, or a support office. There should be a person who is authorized to raise requisitions to avoid staff ordering goods unecessarily.

Requisitions from the production department will be sent to the storekeeper, who will fulfil them internally if possible. If this is done, the storekeeper will raise an *issue note* to confirm that the goods have been issued from stock.

If fresh stocks are required, the storekeeper will issue a requisition to the purchasing officer.

Purchase specification

This gives precise details of the goods to be ordered. The purchasing officer will have a record of previous specifications to help in choosing a supplier. If it is a new request, or the specification has changed, a new specification should be provided.

Quotation

The purchasing officer will contact a number of suppliers to obtain a quotation.

A quotation is a document issued by a supplier, giving details of the price and other terms for supplying the goods requested. Some quotations are made verbally.

The quotations will state the price at which the suppliers are prepared to provide the goods as requested in the purchase specification. The quotations will include:

- basic price as per the specification
- discounts available, e.g. for bulk orders
- delivery costs
- payment terms, e.g. 30-days' credit, cash with order
- any other special terms or procedures

The purchasing officer will examine the quotations and perhaps compile a list of the goods requested and the quotations received. The quotations are then compared and the best one is chosen to supply the goods.

Often, it is the cheapest supplier who wins the order, assuming that the quality, etc. is identical with all the other quotations received. Sometimes though, other suppliers win the order for a variety of reasons. One good reason for accepting a quotation which is not the lowest is to give business to a supplier who we might need in the future, and to keep our name on that supplier's list for special offers, etc. Or we might wish to try a new supplier, even though the quotation given is not the lowest. Or we might give the order to a supplier from whom we are ordering other goods, to keep down our paperwork.

Purchase order

This is a document requesting the goods from the chosen supplier.

Once we have chosen our supplier, we can then place the order. The order might be for several goods at once, and should be in writing wherever possible, as once the supplier has accepted the order it is legally binding.

Official, preprinted order forms should be used, and should be prenumbered to prevent any from being lost, or to prevent staff from ordering goods for themselves. The forms should be in duplicate or triplicate as required – the top copy for the supplier, a copy for the purchasing officer and a copy for head office (if ordering is done locally) or for the branch (if ordering is done centrally).

The order should contain a description of the goods, the quantity required, the price quoted (with any discounts as agreed), delivery terms, and any other relevant items.

All orders should be signed by the purchasing officer.

The copy orders are filed away to await delivery of the goods. Outstanding orders are 'chased up' on a regular basis.

A sample purchase order is shown in Figure 10.1.

Activity 43

Draw up a purchase order from ABC Products Ltd, to Burton and Harris plc, for 100 reams of A4 paper, 80 gsm weight, at £2.40 per ream, less 10% discount, to be delivered in 10 days, free of charge.

Explain briefly the purpose of the purchase order, and how it should be used.

See Feedback section for answer to this activity.

<table>
<tr><td colspan="2">THE PARK HOTEL</td><td colspan="3">PURCHASE ORDER NO. 6347</td></tr>
</table>

THE PARK HOTEL

14 Beach Road
Weaverton
BE1 4XX

Tel: 0663 201499

PURCHASE ORDER NO. 6347

To: Ace Supplies Ltd.

27 Market Street

Northtown

NE2 6ZZ

Date 14/9/94

Quantity	Description	Unit size	Price quoted	Total value
			£	£
50	Tinned Plums	400 gm	0.70	35.00
50	Tinned Tomatoes	250 gm	0.20	10.00

Delivery date required

18/9/94   Signed   P Green   Purchasing Officer

Figure 10.1 A sample purchase order

Receipt of goods

When the goods are received, they must be checked to ensure they are correct. This checking involves several stages and sets of documentation.

The supplier might include a *delivery note* with the goods.

A delivery note is a document issued by the supplier and sent with the goods, giving a description of the goods included in the parcel.

The parcel should be checked to see that it contains the goods as stated on the delivery note. If there is no time to do this, the delivery note should be marked with the words 'goods unseen'. In either case, it should be signed by the person receiving the goods.

Once the goods have been accepted, a *goods received note* is made out. This is a document raised by the purchaser to contain details of the goods received. The delivery note can be used for this purpose, and many organizations do use it, but it is better if the organization uses its own documentation. Suppliers' delivery notes do not necessarily contain the information the organization requires, they are of varying sizes and types, and may contain confusing information. However, using delivery notes does save time in busy organizations, providing that the correct controls are included to provide security and accuracy. Computerized organizations may be able to recall the original order on the computer, and check it with the goods actually received, thereby doing away with the need for a goods received note at all.

The goods received note (GRN) should be prenumbered, to avoid losing any. If delivery notes are used, they should be numbered in sequence. A copy should be kept by the receiving department, and a copy should be passed to the purchasing officer to be compared with the original order. The purchasing officer clips the GRN and original order together.

When the goods have been checked, and any damaged or incorrect items noted, the GRN should be signed and entered in the goods received book in numerical sequence.

A goods received book is a book which lists all the goods received notes issued.

Returns, shortages, damages and incorrect deliveries

If the order contains goods not requested or faulty goods which are to be returned, it is important to ensure that they are not charged for. If the goods are damaged or incorrect, but it is decided to keep them, a reduction in price might be negotiated.

The purchasing officer will arrange for the goods to be returned, will negotiate any reduction in price and will request a credit note.

A credit note is a document issued by a supplier to a buyer, to reduce the amount charged for goods which were damaged, unsuitable, or for which a reduction in price has been agreed for some other reason.

Invoicing

The invoice is the document which the supplier sends to the purchaser, to request payment for the goods delivered.

It might contain items which the organization might not want to pay for, such as goods returned or goods for which a lower price has been agreed; therefore it needs careful checking, for the following:

- to ensure that the goods have been received
- to ensure that goods returned or reduced in price have been adjusted, or a credit note has been issued
- to ensure that the price charged is as stated in the original order
- to ensure that the quantities charged for are correct
- to ensure that any agreed discounts have been given
- to ensure that the invoice has not already been paid

To check these items, the purchasing officer must compare the invoice with the goods received note (which has already been checked with the actual items received, and has details of any goods returned), and the original order. Someone should also check the calculations on the invoice, e.g. totals and VAT – but this might be done by the accounts department. The GRN will be marked with the number of the invoice, so that if another invoice arrives for the same goods it can be queried or rejected. In some cases, the delivery note from the supplier also doubles as an invoice. This is obviously time saving, and perhaps paper saving, but it does mean that any errors on delivery will result in incorrect invoices; in addition, an invoice will be provided for every delivery, so an organization which has many deliveries from the same supplier will have a large number of invoices to deal with.

An example of an invoice is shown in Figure 10.2.

Activity 44

Draw up the invoice which the ABC Products Ltd would receive from Burton and Harris plc, for the goods you ordered in Activity 43. Assume that VAT at 17.5% is to be added to the goods total.

Describe briefly the purpose of an invoice and how it should be used.

See Feedback section for answer to this activity.

Payment

Once the goods have been received and checked to ensure that they are acceptable, we are obliged to pay for them according to the terms agreed.

Ace Supplies Ltd.

27 Market Street
Northtown
NE2 6ZZ

Tel: 0663 204578

To: THE PARK HOTEL
   14 Beach Road
   Weaverton
   BE1 4XX

INVOICE

No: _*P62841*_

Date _*22/9/94*_

Del. note no.	Description of goods	Quantity	Price each £	Total value £
A361	*Tinned Plums*	*50*	*0.70*	*35.00*
A361	*Tinned Tomatoes*	*52*	*0.20*	*10.40*
		Total goods		*45.40*
		Plus VAT @ 17.5%		*–*
		Total invoice		*45.40*

Figure 10.2 A sample invoice

Some suppliers insist on payment with order (e.g. cash and carries), so we might already have paid for these. If there were any faulty goods we will need to obtain a refund.

The majority of suppliers are prepared to wait a short while for payment. Their terms are often noted on the invoice. Some examples of payment terms are:

- nett – this means there is no reduction for prompt payment
- nett, 30 days – this means no reduction for prompt payment and payment is expected within 30 days
- 5% within 10 days – this means that you can deduct 5% discount if you pay within 10 days (or whatever time limit is stated)

Obviously, before any payment is made, we need to ensure that we deduct the total of any credit notes we have received for incorrect goods.

The invoice should be approved for payment by the accounts department.

Investigate 14

Obtain copies of purchasing documentation in use in your own organization. Trace through the documentation for a particular supply of goods or services and check that it is complete. If you have a purchasing manual, compare the procedure it gives with the actual process carried out. Are there any areas of weakness which you could improve upon?

Summary

The purchasing process is an important one in any organization, if only because of the amount of money involved in purchasing the four main types of product – food, liquor, equipment and consumables. You have seen how important it is to choose the correct method of purchasing for each type of product, because each method has its own characteristics. Some may be of advantage to the organization, but others may not, and mistakes can be very costly and difficult to correct.

You have also seen how the various stages in the purchasing process form part of a continuous system of control to ensure that the correct goods are requested, ordered, delivered and paid for at the correct price. Mistakes here can also be expensive ones. Goods can be mislaid or delivered incorrectly and in poor condition, and hence will be of no use to the organization. The control procedures included in the documents and records, together with proper authorization and physical checks, ensure that mistakes are few and are quickly located and corrected.

RESOURCES MANAGEMENT

Review and discussion questions

1 What things would you consider before choosing a source of supply for a particular product?
2 List the main methods of purchasing.
3 What are the advantages and disadvantages of each method of purchasing?
4 What information would you find on a purchase specification?

5 List the stages in the purchasing process, with a brief description of the activities which take place, and the documents used at each stage.

Case study

Bennet and Sons plc manufacture sweets and confectionery for sale to retailers. The machinery is old and some is in need of replacement. They also need to update their computer information system. As well as purchases of sugar, chocolate and other ingredients, they also require large quantities of boxes and other packaging materials.

There are five factories throughout the country. The accounting function is carried out at a central location, so stationery requirements there are substantial.

Identify a range of products and services which Bennet and Sons might require, and the most appropriate method of purchasing these. Write a short report to the company outlining the reasons for your choice.

Draw up a document which outlines the documentation required in purchasing, for staff to have on hand.

Work-based assignment

B1.1
B1.2

Identify four products or services which your organization buys. Draw up specifications for these, and locate suppliers and methods by which they might be acquired. Evaluate the methods currently in use and suggest alternatives.

PURCHASING OF GOODS AND SERVICES

11 Recording and control of stocks, labour and fixed assets

Learning objectives

On completion of this chapter you will be able to:

- maintain stock records
- value stocks using three common valuation methods
- understand the difficulties of stock valuation
- calculate the gross wages of an employee using two common methods
- understand the various ways in which employees are rewarded
- use documentation to record labour activities
- assess the productivity and efficiency of labour
- appreciate the need to record and control fixed assets

Introduction

As well as ensuring that resources are purchased in the right manner, it is important that they are recorded and controlled while they are in the organization. This chapter looks at methods of recording and measuring the availability, use and efficiency of stocks, labour and fixed assets.

Control of stocks

Stocks can constitute a great deal of investment in some organizations, and hence it is important that they are properly controlled. Control is necessary to ensure that stocks are:

- available when required for production or sale
- kept in appropriate storage conditions
- accessible to those who need them
- safeguarded from theft or damage
- valued accurately to ensure as precise a measure as possible of the costs

Controls over the movement of stocks

It is important that the organization knows what has happened to its stocks. In a manufacturing organization many different types of raw materials come in, perhaps to a general store area. From there they might be passed to a production area, and then onto individual jobs or production lines.

As the production proceeds, there might be various outputs from the process, such as byproducts which go on to other processes, or waste materials which might be saleable.

The items produced might go on to other departments for finishing or including with other products.

There will be stocks of partly finished goods, and of finished items. The finished goods may already be allocated to a customer's order, or they may be produced in anticipation of future orders.

You can see that there are several different occasions where stock movements need to be controlled and recorded. It is important that every movement is properly authorized.

Documents used in the control of stocks

You have seen in the previous chapter that various documents are used in the purchasing process. Some of these can be used in the control of stocks. The goods received note, for example, can be used as evidence of raw materials purchased and added to stock, although it might be the invoice that gives details of the cost. Returns notes and credit notes provide evidence of stocks being returned to the supplier.

Once materials are recorded in the stock records, *issue notes* are used to record their movement within the organization. There will also be various documents used during production to identify the stage at which stocks are at. These are not covered in this book.

Many organizations compile two types of stock record:

1 **The bin card**
This records *quantities* of goods received and issued, and the resulting balance, and is often kept with the goods themselves so that the storekeeper can see the situation, and take action if necessary.

2 **The stock record card**
This records *values* of stocks as well as quantities. This is often maintained by the purchasing department or accounts department.

RECORDING AND CONTROL OF STOCKS, LABOUR AND FIXED ASSETS

Bear in mind that in many organizations, these records are computerized, and the details are available through the computer rather than as physical documents.

Ensuring the accuracy of stock records

Organizations are well advised not to rely entirely on their records to determine the level of stock. Mistakes can be made in all recording systems, and the actual level of stock may differ from that recorded. It is important to carry out a *physical stock check* to verify the amount of stock as compared with the records. This might be done on a continuous basis, on all stock lines, periodically on selected stock lines, or annually as part of the audit procedures.

Minor differences between the physical count and the records, provided the items are of relatively low value, and provided that the differences do not arise frequently, are often ignored as it is too time consuming to determine the reasons for the differences. Larger, frequently occurring differences, or differences in high-value items should always be investigated.

If actual stock is greater than that recorded, this is not as worrying as stock which is less than recorded, but should still be investigated if necessary. Actual stock which is less than the recorded amount could be due to:

- incorrect calculations on the bin card
- an issue to production which has been omitted or recorded wrongly
- a purchase which has been recorded wrongly
- goods returned which have been omitted

Methods of valuing stocks

The accounting profession follows the rule that stocks should be valued at the lower of their cost, or their 'net realizable value'. Net realizable value is the value which could be obtained for the stocks in their present condition, less any extra cost to be incurred in making them saleable.

The value placed on the stocks will affect the calculation of cost of goods sold (and hence the profit) and the value as shown on the balance sheet as an asset.

RESOURCES MANAGEMENT

The problem which faces the accountant is: what is the cost of the stock?

The question is easily answered if the items in stock throughout the year were all bought at the same price, or, if there are only a few items of stock used in the year, for specific orders.

But many organizations are not so lucky. They are buying in different quantities of stocks throughout the year, and at different prices, and using them as they are required. Most new stocks are placed at the front of the shelf, or on the top of the bin, even though there are older stocks at the back. They are removed from the shelves in no particular order. It would be too time consuming to label each item of stock with its cost, and in many cases that level of precision is not necessary. With increasing use of computers, many organizations are now using barcodes to mark their stocks, so that each item can be scanned as it is used, and an accurate record kept of its value. Barcodes and other aspects of computerization are discussed in the book entitled *Information Management*.

Consider the following example, to illustrate the problem.

On 1 January, there are 20 items in stock which cost £10 each – total value £200

On 8 January, 20 more items are purchased, costing £12 each – total value £240

On 15 January, 20 items are sold for £15 each

What is the value of the 20 items which have been sold? How much profit has been made on them? What is the value of the 20 items remaining?

There are several possible answers to these questions.

1 When the new items were purchased, they were put at the front of the shelf, so they were the ones sold to the customer. They cost £12 each, so the value of the stock sold was £240. As they were sold for £15 each, the profit was £3 on each one – total £60. The value of the stock remaining is £200.

2 The storekeeper exercises good housekeeping, and picked out the older stock for sale to the customer. They cost £10 each, so the value of stock sold was £200. They were sold for £15 each, so the profit was £5 on each one – total £100. The value of the stock remaining is £240.

3 The storekeeper chooses at random the items to sell. He might choose 10 old items and 10 new, or any combination. How would we value stock then?

4 We might decide to use an 'average' value of £11 each for the stock. This is easily calculated as we had equal quantities costing £10 and £12 – so the middle value is £11. This gets rather more complicated, though, if we have different quantities and prices involved.

It is obvious that the organization needs to choose a particular method which suits its needs, and is reasonably convenient. The method chosen might reflect the true way in which the stocks are used, or more likely it will be based on the *assumption* that stocks are used in a particular way, even if they aren't.

We will look at three common methods of valuing stocks.

The following example of stock movements of Material X is used to illustrate the three common methods of stock valuation covered in this chapter:

1 July	Opening stock	10 items @ £10 each
13 July	Purchases	5 items @ £16 each
20 July	Issues	8 items
25 July	Issues	3 items
30 July	Purchases	12 items @ £18 each

The first in first out (FIFO) method

This method assumes that the stocks which were received first are issued (used) first. Thus stocks remaining at the end of the period are assumed to be those which were received most recently.

The stock record card using the FIFO method would appear as shown in Figure 11.1.

The balance is restated after each transaction, and after each issue a line is drawn across to show the new balance. So, the purchase on 13 July resulted in *two* values of stock on hand. The issue on 20 July was of the earliest items at £10 each; this left a balance of two items at £10 plus five items at £16. The issue on 25 July consisted of items at both values because there were not enough of the £10 items to satisfy the issue. The final balance consists of two values of stock, totalling £280.

	Receipts			Issues			Balance		
	Qty	Value each	Total value	Qty	Value each	Total value	Qty	Value each	Total value
		£	£		£	£		£	£
1 July							10	10.00	100.00
13 July	5	16.00	80.00				5	16.00	80.00
20 July				8	10.00	80.00	2	10.00	20.00
							5	16.00	80.00
25 July				2	10.00				
				1	16.00	36.00	4	16.00	64.00
30 July	12	18.00	216.00				12	18.00	216.00
TOTALS	Receipts		296.00	Issues		116.00	Balance		280.00

Figure 11.1 Stock record card using FIFO method

The last in first out (LIFO) method

This method assumes that the stocks which were received most recently are issued first. Thus stocks remaining at the end of the period are assumed to be those which were received earliest.

The stock record card using the LIFO method would appear as shown in Figure 11.2.

This time, the issue on 20 July consisted of items at both values; the £16 items are issued first, but as there are only five of them it is assumed that three of the £10 items are issued too.

Comparing the closing stock value with the FIFO method indicates that, in times of rising prices, the FIFO method gives a higher closing stock value than the LIFO method, and hence a lower cost of goods sold figure and a higher profit figure. For this reason, the Inland Revenue will not accept the LIFO method as a valid method, and therefore it is less popular.

	Receipts			Issues			Balance		
	Qty	Value each	Total value	Qty	Value each	Total value	Qty	Value each	Total value
		£	£		£	£		£	£
1 July							10	10.00	100.00
13 July	5	16.00	80.00				5	16.00	80.00
20 July				5	16.00				
				3	10.00	110.00	7	10.00	70.00
25 July				3	10.00	30.00	4	10.00	40.00
30 July	12	18.00	216.00				12.00	18.00	216.00
TOTALS	Receipts		296.00	Issues		140.00	Balance		256.00

Figure 11.2 Stock record card using LIFO method

The average cost (AVCO) method

This method calculates a new 'average cost' each time a purchase is made. This average cost is then used for all issues, until another purchase is made. In times of rising prices, this results in stocks values which are rising but which are in between the FIFO and LIFO methods. It appears to be a sensible compromise but it does mean that a new average needs to be calculated with each purchase.

The stock record card using the AVCO method would appear as shown in Figure 11.3.

Thus, when a new purchase is made, for example on 13 July, a new average cost is calculated. The total value of £180 is divided by the total quantity of 15, to give an average cost of £12 each. This value is then used for the issues on 20 July and 25 July. When another purchase is made on 30 July the new average cost becomes £264 divided by 16 = £16.50.

	Receipts			Issues			Balance		
	Qty	Value each	Total value	Qty	Value each	Total value	Qty	Value each	Total value
		£	£		£	£		£	£
1 July							10	10.00	100.00
13 July	5	16.00	80.00				15	12.00	180.00
20 July				8	12.00	96.00	7	12.00	84.00
25 July				3	12.00	36.00	4	12.00	48.00
30 July	12	18.00	216.00				16.00	16.50	264.00
TOTALS	Receipts		296.00	Issues		132.00	Balance		264.00

Figure 11.3 Stock record card using AVCO method

Activity 45

From the following data, draw up a stock record card using the three methods of stock valuation shown above, i.e. FIFO, LIFO and AVCO.

  1 April   100 units on hand, valued at £10 each
  8 April   24 units sold
18 April   38 units purchased for £456
20 April   50 units sold
23 April   35 units sold
28 April   20 units purchased for £260

See Feedback section for answer to this activity.

Reducing the cost of materials

Reductions in costs are possible, but usually there are disadvantages to all cost reduction attempts.

Bulk purchasing may give discounts, but additional storage is required, and the goods have to be paid for sooner than if they were bought in smaller quantities over a longer period.

RECORDING AND CONTROL OF STOCKS, LABOUR AND FIXED ASSETS

Advantage should be taken of special offers and promotions, as well as carrying out a thorough search for the best deal from a selection of suppliers.

Buying lower grade materials might result in increased wastage or slower machine running times. Buying higher grade materials might actually improve performance.

Buying materials in different sizes might also be cost effective. It is not always the case that larger sizes are cheaper. If a single piece of material is used to provide several smaller pieces, care should be taken to choose the size and shape which best fits the requirements.

Control of labour

The textbook *People and Self Management* covers aspects of managing the work force. This book looks at methods of recording and controlling workers' activities, calculating the cost of the work force, and calculating wages and salaries.

The cost of labour

There are many different ways in which employees are rewarded for their services, and they all have some cost to the organization. Some of these are as follows:

- basic wages or salary
- bonuses related to output
- profit sharing schemes
- sickness and holiday payments
- benefits in kind (perks), such as cars, medical insurance, mobile telephones
- employer contributions to pension schemes
- discounts on company products and services
- provision of sports facilities
- subsidized canteens
- childcare facilities

As well as all the ancillary costs of employing staff such as the human resources department, the wages department, and so on. In addition, there are costs involved in making wage payments, such as national insurance contributions.

This book does not cover all of these, but it is important that you appreciate that the cost of employing a person is far more than just calculating a wage or salary. It is particularly important to consider how your organization deals with absence for whatever reason. If an employee is normally paid £10,000 a year for a five-day week, this equates to 260 working days a year. But if the employee is allowed 20 days' holiday, and an average employee takes 10 days off for sickness, training, etc., then the working days are only 230. This will affect the cost you use in any calculations.

Investigate 15	What facilities and rewards does your own organization provide to its employees apart from their salaries?

'Fixed' and 'flexible' reward systems

Some employees may be paid a fixed amount each week or month, irrespective of the level of activity or output they produce. This may be enhanced by an annual bonus, but the basic pay is essentially fixed, and produces the same gross pay each week or month, before deductions are considered.

Flexible systems allow for different amounts to be paid according to the work done. There are two main types of flexible system.

Time-based systems

These reward employees according to the amount of time they have spent at work. There may be a daily or hourly rate, which is multiplied by the number of days or hours worked. The employee might be required to do a certain number of hours each day or week, and then might be paid extra for additional hours. This is known as *overtime*. Some employers pay the same rate for overtime as for normal time; some pay extra, e.g. time and a half, which means that the rate is the basic rate plus one half. There may be even larger amounts paid for weekend working or work on bank holidays.

172

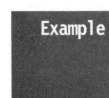

Example

Howard is paid £5 per hour for a basic 40-hour week, with overtime at basic rate plus 50%. During Week 8, he worked 46 hours. His gross wage would be:

40 hours at £5 per hour	£200.00
6 hours at £7.50 per hour	£ 45.00
Total gross wages	£245.00

Output-based systems

Output-based wages are based on the level of output or number of items produced, again with a higher rate for larger numbers to improve productivity. This method is sometimes called the 'piece work' method.

Example

Shirley is paid £1 per item for up to 150 items, and £2 per item thereafter. During Week 8, she produces 200 items. Her gross wage would be:

150 items @ £1 each	£150.00
50 items @ £2 each	£100.00
Total gross wages	£245.00

There is often a minimum wage with this method, to avoid the situation where productivity is low due to no fault of the employee, for example because of machinery breakdown or the slowness of other operators on whom the employee relies.

Activity 46

Calculate the gross wages for the following employee, using both time-based and output-based methods:

Hours worked   – 45; basic rate £3 per hour, with hours above 40 at time and a half

Units produced – 400; basic rate 25p per unit up to 300; 50p per unit above 300

See Feedback section for answer to this activity.

RESOURCES MANAGEMENT

Recording time spent

There are many different ways in which time can be recorded. Some employers simply require evidence that the employee has attended on a particular day. This can be done by providing a system of 'clocking in', whereby a machine or computer records the time the employee arrives and departs. Some organizations do this by getting employees to 'sign in' and 'sign out'. This can be useful even where pay is not dependant on the time spent.

However, more detailed records of how time has been spent might be required.

Time sheets

Time sheets are one such type of record. The employee keeps a daily record of the work done. An example is shown in Figure 11.4.

TIME SHEET

Name: *Freda Bloggs*　　　　Employee No. *456*　　　　Week No. *23*

Hours spent

	Job 125	Job 78	Job 904	Meetings	Other	Details
Monday	4.00	3.00				
Tuesday	4.00		2.00	1.00		
Wednesday					7.00	Holiday
Thursday		5.00		2.00		
Friday	3.00	2.00	2.00			
Totals	11.00	10.00	4.00	3.00	7.00	35.00

Figure 11.4 An example time sheet

A daily time sheet might be necessary if more detail than this is needed.

A solicitor, for example, might record a day's activities as shown in Figure 11.5.

Job sheets

These bring together the costs for each job or activity. They will include the costs of materials and overheads, as well as labour, but initially the labour costs will be summarized

Monday 23rd March xxx1			
	Activity	**Hours**	**Client Ref**
08.30–9.00	Opening post	0.50	
09.00–10.00	Discussions with partner	1.00	
10.00–10.15	Phone to Mrs Baker re letter in post	0.25	B12
10.15–10.45	Interview with new client, J. Turner	0.50	T45
10.45–12.00	Visit to bank re overdraft facilities	1.25	
12.00–1.00	Dictate letter to opposition re Ms Jones	1.00	J57
2.00–2.30	Phone from P. Hull re house move	0.50	H81
2.30–3.30	Analysing outstanding debts	1.00	
3.30–4.00	Interview with E. Smith	0.50	S24
4.00–5.00	Dictate letter to Mrs Baker	1.00	B12
5.00–6.00	Reading new law on leasing	1.00	

Figure 11.5 A daily time sheet

Labour record			
Job No. 125			**Week No. 23**
Employee	**Hours**	**Rate £**	**Cost £**
456.00	11.00	5.50	60.50
801.00	8.00	6.00	48.00
209.00	10.00	6.20	62.00
575.00	24.00	5.00	120.00

Figure 11.6 An example job sheet

separately. Freda Bloggs, Employee Number 456, as you saw earlier, worked on Job Number 125 for 11 hours in Week 23. Other employees might also have worked on that job, so the job sheet might look like that shown in Figure 11.6.

From this the total cost of labour on this job can be determined as time goes on.

Labour efficiency measures

As well as calculating the cost of labour, an organization might need to measure the efficiency of its work force. The types of measures will depend on the nature of the work involved.

Production labour

Efficiency measurements will be based mainly on output produced.

The total number of units produced during a week   10,000
Direct labour hours used in production   500

$$\text{Production efficiency per unit} = \frac{\text{labour hours used}}{\text{units produced}}$$

$$= \frac{500}{10,000} = 0.05 \text{ hours per unit}$$

or

$$\text{Production efficiency per hour} = \frac{\text{units produced}}{\text{hours used}}$$

$$= \frac{10,000}{500} = 20 \text{ units per hour}$$

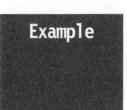

The number of units produced during a week is normally 25 units per hour. If only 20 units per hour are produced, then the efficiency could be expressed as:

$$\frac{\text{actual units produced}}{\text{normal units produced}} \times 100 = \frac{20}{25} = 80\%$$

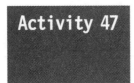

Activity 47

Calculate the labour efficiency for a group of workers who produce 4,000 units in 200 hours. The normal level of production is 18 per hour.

See Feedback section for answer to this activity.

Administrative labour

Measures here could include the following:

- for a secretary – the number of letters per hour
- for a salesperson – the number of sales per day
- for a lecturer – the number of hours teaching per week
- for a care assistant – the number of home visits per week
- for a surgeon – the number of operations per week
- for a customer service department – the number of complaints handled per week

Efficiency measures for all labour

It is unlikely that all workers will be 'productive' every minute of every day. Reasons why this is so will vary from job to job, but examples could include:

- rest breaks
- 'switch over' time between jobs
- machine breakdowns
- lateness
- absence through illness
- holidays
- attending meetings and discussions
- training themselves
- training others

The amount of time spent in these activities should also be measured and monitored. It is widely accepted that absenteeism, for example, costs organizations several millions of pounds per year – the actual amount is unknown mainly because organizations do not properly monitor it.

Reducing labour costs

Few employees are likely to accept a cut in wages, so other methods of reducing labour costs need to be considered.

RESOURCES MANAGEMENT

Many organizations are tending to use temporary staff on short-term contracts, rather than permanent staff. Although the actual wages might not be reduced, the costs of redundancy and sickness might be. Part-time staff and staff prepared to work flexible hours are also useful as they can be hired as required.

Improving productivity of staff might cost extra, but if the output is improved to produce additional profit, this should cover the extra cost. This would then mean that fewer staff are required.

Training staff in new methods of working, or updating existing skills, should ensure that staff are performing their jobs correctly. Training can also improve motivation, reduce absenteeism, and hence improve productivity.

The use of technology in routine and repetitive tasks can improve speed and accuracy, enabling staffing levels to be reduced or staff released to be redeployed in other areas.

Control of fixed assets

Fixed assets involve considerable long-term investment by organizations. It is important that their usage is monitored and controlled.

The cost of fixed assets

As well as the cost of purchasing or building fixed assets, there will be many other costs incurred, whether on a regular or intermittent basis.

The initial capital cost will include delivery and installation costs. There might also be training costs for new assets, and consequently lower production until staff have familiarized themselves with new methods and procedures.

Ongoing costs will include the following:

- regular maintenance
- ad hoc maintenance and breakdown
- cost of hiring replacements
- lost production during maintenance and breakdown
- insurance
- power costs
- consumables, e.g. stationery for a computer system
- security systems
- financing costs for loans, mortgages, etc.

Recording systems for fixed assets

Apart from recording the *costs* of fixed assets, there are other items of information which need to be available. One of the biggest problems with smaller fixed assets is in knowing where they are! Portable items of equipment, such as computers, can be moved about from department to department – and between home and work – without anyone keeping track of them. One day, the item is badly needed and it cannot be found!

Even if the item is located, it might not be in working order, because it has not been used for some time, or because the person last using it did not report it as broken.

There are also instances of fixed assets being purchased which are never used.

There are various methods of recording information on fixed assets. One is to maintain a *fixed asset register*. This might show the following data for each asset:

- description
- date of purchase
- cost
- depreciation record
- supplier
- insurance details
- location
- breakdown and maintenance record
- usage, e.g. number of hours, miles travelled, units produced

Controls over the use of fixed assets

Fixed assets should not be moved around without authority and notification. Every fixed asset should be labelled with a code, and for more expensive items, a non-removable label detailing ownership.

Regular physical checks should be made on the existence of fixed assets. These should be done without warning on smaller items to avoid the possibility of employees returning fixed assets which they have taken home, awaiting the physical check, and then taking them home again.

Equipment should, wherever possible, be fixed to prevent its removal, and appropriate security measures taken such as locking doors and using security cameras. Some items of equipment can be fitted with an individual alarm which detects movement.

Efficiency measures for fixed assets

As with labour, there are various ways of measuring the efficiency of fixed assets. Here are some examples:

- for a building
  - number of opening hours
  - number of employees per square metre of floor space
  - cost of heat and light per cubic metre
- for a computer - number of items processed
- for a production machine - number of units produced, per hour
- for a car - number of business miles per year
- for a lorry - number of deliveries per week
- for a football pitch - number of spectators per week

Summary

Now that you have completed this chapter you should understand the importance of recording the usage of stocks, labour and fixed assets. You should be able to complete stock record cards using three methods of stock valuation. You should be able to assess the efficiency of staff in the organization by the calculation of efficiency measures. You should appreciate the need for control over fixed assets to ensure their availability when required and in fit condition.

Review and discussion questions

1 Why is it important to keep control of stocks? What dangers are there in not keeping proper records?
2 What documents are used in the control of stocks?
3 What are the three main methods of stocks valuation and how do they differ?
4 How might materials costs be reduced?
5 What are the costs involved in employing staff?
6 What documents are used in the recording and control of labour?
7 How might labour costs be reduced?
8 What information might you find in a fixed asset register?

Case study

Martin has recently been appointed Assistant Factory Manager with a small manufacturing business. He is concerned to find that there are several problems which are affecting production and preventing management from fully understanding the costs which are being incurred.

Stock records are maintained on bin cards, but only in quantity terms. The account's office values stock at whatever the price was at the previous year end, of 31 December.

Employees are currently paid on a time basis, and have complained that this is unfair when some workers are more productive than others. They have asked that a new system be considered which rewards those who produce more.

The Factory Manager moves workers around from job to job during the day, and has no mechanism for recording hours spent on each job.

Write a memo to the Factory Manager, outlining the following:

- three methods of valuing stocks
- a method of rewarding workers who produce more
- a mechanism for recording time spent on each job.

Work-based assignment

B1.1
B1.2

Draw up a document to record your time spent at work. Divide your time between the various duties you perform. Calculate the proportion spent on activities you consider to be 'productive' and those which are 'non-productive', such as attending meetings.

12 Decision making

Learning objectives

On completion of this chapter you will be able to:

- calculate the financial effects of short-term decisions
- appreciate the financial effects of short-term decisions
- consider implications other than financial ones on short-term decisions
- understand how short-term decisions can have a long-term impact
- calculate the financial effects of long-term decisions
- appreciate the need to analyse costs and benefits in long-term decisions

Introduction

Managers make decisions daily. Some of these decisions have only a short-term impact on the organization, and often have to be taken quickly; others have a long-term impact and may take several weeks or months to be made.

This chapter looks at a range of decisions, both short and long term, and some of the techniques which can be used in making them.

It is important to remember that the *financial* impact of decisions is not the only factor to take into account, but is only one consideration of many.

In making decisions, there are several questions which can be asked, which might affect the information required to make the decision. These include:

1 Is the present capacity of the organization being used to its fullest?
2 Does the decision depend on availability of resources, such as materials and labour?
3 Will the decision affect existing operations?
4 Are there alternatives which could be considered?
5 Could a short-term decision have repercussions in the long term?
6 Do the benefits of the decision outweigh the costs?
7 Is the information on which the decision is based certain, or is there a degree of uncertainty?

Accepting special orders

It might happen that your organization gets a request for a special, one-off order.

In general, if you are able to fulfil the order using your present capacity, with no requirement for additional fixed costs, and the order provides some *contribution*, then it should be accepted on financial grounds.

In particular, if the organization has not yet achieved *break-even point*, most orders which provide a contribution should be accepted.

Operating below break-even point

Your firm has regular monthly orders for 1,000 units of Product A, with a selling price of £20 each and variable costs of £12. Each unit, therefore contributes £8 (remember that *contribution* is the selling price less the variable costs). Fixed costs are £10,000 per annum.

$$\text{Break-even point} = \frac{\text{Fixed costs}}{\text{Contribution per unit}}$$

$$= \frac{£10,000}{£8} = 1,250 \text{ units}$$

With orders for only 1,000 units, break-even point has not yet been reached.

If an additional order is received for 100 units, selling for £15, this should be accepted, since it will bring in additional contribution of £3 per unit – that is £300 extra towards the fixed costs.

Of course, you need to confirm that you have sufficient labour available, but this is likely if you are operating below break-even point.

Operating above break-even point, but below full capacity

Your firm has the capacity to produce 5,000 units a month. Existing customers take up 4,000 units a month. Selling price is normally £30, with variable costs of £18. Fixed costs are £40,000 per month.

$$\text{Break-even point} = \frac{\text{Fixed costs}}{\text{Contribution per unit}}$$

$$= \frac{\pounds 36,000}{\pounds 12} = 3,000 \text{ units}$$

Existing customers already cover fixed costs, and contribute towards the profit:

	£
Contribution at present (4,000 x £12)	48,000
Fixed costs	36,000
Profit	12,000

A new customer requests 500 units at a price of £25 each. Variable costs are still £18 a unit, so the new order will contribute £7 a unit, giving a total of £3,500 extra profit, i.e.

		£
Contribution at present		48,000
Contribution from new order	3,500	
Total contribution		51,500
Fixed costs		36,000
Profit		15,500

As the firm is already operating at a profit, it might need to consider the possible impact of this new order on existing customers, if they discover that you have accepted a much lower selling price for this order. If all customers demanded the same selling price of £25 a unit, you need to calculate the impact of this on profits:

	£
Contribution from 4,500 units at £7 each	31,500
Fixed costs	36,000
Loss	4,500

The break-even point is now much higher:

$$\text{Revised break-even point} = \frac{\text{Fixed costs}}{\text{Contribution per unit}}$$

$$= \frac{\pounds 36,000}{\pounds 7} = 5,143 \text{ units}$$

Obviously, this situation is not acceptable, and the new order should be refused if this is the likely outcome.

Activity 48

A firm has regular orders for 2,500 units, with full capacity of 3,000 units. Selling price is normally £50 a unit, with variable costs of £30, and fixed costs of £40,000. A new customer has requested 500 units at a price of £40 each. Calculate the effects of accepting the new order, and discuss the implications.

See Feedback section for answer to this activity.

Operating at full capacity

If the firm is already operating at full capacity, there are several options which could be considered. Some of these are:

- cut existing production to satisfy the new order
- buy in the additional units for the new order
- expand operations to accommodate the order

Cutting existing production to satisfy the new order

A firm currently manufactures and sells 1,000 units a month, working at full capacity. Selling price is £40 a unit, variable costs are £25 a unit, and fixed costs are £10,000. A new order is received for 200 units at a price of £36.

The new order brings in additional contribution, but if the firm has to cut existing production it will lose the contribution from those units, which is greater than that from the new order.

	£
Additional contribution (200 × £11)	2,200
Lost contribution (200 × £15)	3,000
Reduction in profit	800

On financial grounds, the decision should be not to fulfil this order. The existing customers whose orders are not fulfilled might never return. On the other hand, it might be that the new order is expected to be repeated or increased in the future; the new customer might be one which the firm has sought for some time, and is offering this low price as an introductory price only, to be raised with future orders.

This short-term decision might have long-term implications, and should be made with caution.

Buy in the additional units for the new order

Using the same example as above, suppose it is possible to buy in the extra units for £28 a unit. Selling price is £36, so contribution of £8 per unit will be provided by the new order, with no change to existing operations and contribution.

Additional contribution = 200 × £8

= £1,600 extra profit

Again, existing customers might respond negatively if they discover this reduced price is available, and you need to consider the possible impact of that. In addition, buying in products always carries the risk of lower quality or delivery problems which are outside your control.

Expand operations

It might be possible to expand operations by providing extra space or machinery. This obviously carries extra fixed costs. Suppose that extra capacity of 400 units a month could be provided if another machine were purchased at a cost of £10,000. The machine is expected to last for 10 years, so annual depreciation would be £1,000.

	£
Additional contribution (200 × £11)	2,200
Extra fixed costs	1,000
Increase in profit	1,200

Based on these results, this would be an acceptable option, with the added benefit of a further 200 units able to be produced from the new machine. However, if the new order is only a one-off occurrence and is not repeated, the machine might lie idle for the next 10 years, with depreciation of £1,000 per year as an extra fixed cost. This is another example of a short-term decision having long-term implications.

Activity 49

A firm currently manufactures and sells 2,000 units a month, working at full capacity. Selling price is £30 a unit, variable costs are £20 a unit, and fixed costs are £12,000. A new order is received for 200 units at a price of £26.

The firm is operating at full capacity. It could buy in the extra units for £25, cut existing production to supply the order, or expand operations with a new machine costing £5,000 and expected to last for 10 years.

Calculate the possible effects of these three alternatives and consider your results.

See Feedback section for answer to this activity.

Make or buy decisions

A firm might have the option to either make goods itself, or buy them in from outside.

Suppose that a firm makes several components which go into a single product. Component X has the following costs:

	£
Direct materials	20
Direct labour	35
Variable overheads	10
Fixed overheads	25
	90

An outside supplier can provide the component for £80. From this information, it would seem better to buy in the component.

But you need to consider what would happen to the fixed overheads. If they would disappear, then the decision is simple. But if they would remain, for example if they consist of premises rental which is still to be paid, then a different picture is presented. The true cost of buying in the component would be the £80 purchase price *plus* the fixed overheads of £25 – i.e. £105. So buying in the component would cost £15 more than making it.

This can be shown by considering only the variable costs:

	£
Variable costs of manufacture	65
Cost of buying in	80
Difference	15

Activity 50

Your firm makes a component with the following costs:

	£
Direct materials	25
Direct labour	15
Variable overheads	5
Fixed overheads	20
	65

An outside supplier can provide the component for £60. Should you make the component or buy it in?

See Feedback section for answer to this activity.

Deleting a product

If an organization makes several products, the fixed costs will be apportioned to each of them in some way. This might mean that some products appear to make more profit than others, depending on the method of apportionment.

Suppose that a firm makes three components:

	A £	B £	C £	TOTAL £
Sales	7,000	10,000	8,000	25,000
Variable costs	3,000	4,000	6,000	13,000
Contribution	4,000	6,000	2,000	12,000
Fixed costs	2,500	2,500	3,000	8,000
Profit/(Loss)	1,500	3,500	(1,000)	4,000

On these figures, it would seem sensible to cease production of Component C, as it makes a loss. However, the decision depends on what happens to the fixed costs apportioned to Component C. If they still remain, then they will have to be apportioned to the other two components. The result of that would be as follows:

	A £	B £	TOTAL £
Sales	7,000	10,000	17,000
Variable costs	3,000	4,000	7,000
Contribution	4,000	6,000	10,000
Fixed costs	4,000	4,000	8,000
Profit	nil	2,000	2,000

DECISION MAKING

Far from making a saving, the profit has gone down by £2,000. This is because component C made a *contribution* of £2,000 to the fixed costs.

The decision might be different if the surplus capacity released by dropping component C could be used on the other components.

Activity 51

Suppose that a firm makes three components:

	A £	B £	C £	TOTAL £
Sales	4,000	6,000	5,000	15,000
Variable costs	2,000	2,000	4,000	8,000
Contribution	2,000	4,000	1,000	7,000
Fixed costs	1,500	1,500	1,500	4,500
Profit/(Loss)	500	2,500	(500)	2,500

Calculate the effects of ceasing production of component C.

See Feedback section for answer to this activity.

Reducing production where resources are limited

If there is a shortage of resources, this is known as a *limiting factor*. It prevents the firm from producing all the items it would like. In such cases, it will be necessary to reduce or cease production of one or more items, even if they are all profitable.

Suppose a firm makes three products:

	A	B	C
Selling price per unit	£20	£30	£40
Variable cost per unit	£10	£12	£28
Machine hours per unit	2	4	3
Demand	10,000	6,000	12,000

Machine capacity is limited to 65,000 hours.

The decision involves three stages.

Stage 1 – determine how many machine hours are currently required

	A	B	C
Machine hours per unit	2	4	3
Demand	10,000	6,000	12,000
Total hours required	20,000	24,000	36,000

Total machine hours required are 80,000. Therefore there is a shortfall of 15,000 hours.

Stage 2 – determine the contribution from each product

	A	B	C
Selling price per unit	£20	£30	£40
Variable cost per unit	£10	£12	£28
Contribution per unit	£10	£18	£12

At the stage you might think that product A should be reduced, as it produces the lowest contribution. But product A only uses two hours of machine time, so 7,500 would have to be dropped from production – this would lose £75,000 in contribution (7,500 @ £10 each). The other two products use more machine time, so maybe one of those should be dropped instead.

Stage 3 – determine the contribution per unit of scare resource

The scarce resource is machine hours. The contribution *per machine hour* for each of the products is as follows:

	A	B	C
Contribution per unit	£10	£18	£12
Machine hours per unit	2	4	3
Contribution per machine hour	£5	£4.50	£4

Product C produces the lowest contribution per machine hour, so should be the first choice to be reduced or dropped. Product A makes the most efficient use of machine time, so would be the last choice to be dropped.

We can now determine how many of each product to make, to make best use of machine time:

	Production quantity	Machine hours per unit	Total machine hours
Product A	10,000	2	20,000
Product B	6,000	4	24,000
Product C	7,000	3	21,000 (balance)

The production quantity for product C takes up the balance of 21,000 hours, so at 3 hours per unit, 7,000 can be produced. 5,000 have had to be dropped, losing contribution of £60,000.

Activity 52

Suppose a firm makes three products:

	A	B	C
Selling price per unit	£30	£40	£50
Variable cost per unit	£5	£25	£30
Machine hours per unit	10	5	4
Demand	2,000	3,000	4,000

Machine capacity is limited to 48,000 hours.

Calculate the effects of reducing production of one of the products. Which would you choose to reduce and why?

See Feedback section for answer to this activity.

Investment decisions

When an organization decides to invest in a long-term project, it needs to be able to convince itself and any other investors of the wisdom of that investment. A wrong decision can have effects which last for a very long time. It needs to be sure that the benefits of the investment will exceed the costs.

There are many difficulties in making long-term investment decisions. One is that forecasting far into the future is always uncertain and carries a degree of risk of inaccuracy. Another is that not all costs and benefits can be anticipated in advance. A third is that it is not always possible to place a value on costs and benefits – some are *unquantifiable*.

Finally, a major difficulty in dealing with the future is that money values change as time goes on. £1 today will not have the same purchasing power as £1 in the future. This is known as the *time value of money*. You can imagine this as meaning the effects of inflation on money values, but it can also be viewed as the lost benefit of being able to invest the money in something else which produces an income. This is known as the firm's *discount rate* or *cost of capital*.

Identifying the costs

The costs of a long-term project are similar to those involved in the acquisition of fixed assets. They include not only the cost of purchasing assets, but a variety of additional costs such as legal fees, surveyors' and architects' fees and installation costs.

Other costs might include training, and lost production during any changeover or development.

Ongoing costs might include running costs, stationery, insurance, etc.

Unquantifiable costs might include staff resistance to change.

Identifying the benefits

The most easily identified benefits will be additional profits and/or cash flows generated by the investment. Other benefits might include improved speed of throughput, improved accuracy, less wastage, enhanced staff morale and even improved information and decision making. Several of these are unquantifiable.

Comparing the quantifiable costs and benefits

There are three main methods of comparing the quantifiable costs and benefits. These are:

1 the payback period
2 the accounting rate of return
3 the net present value of future cash flows

This section looks at each of these, using the following example:

A firm wishes to invest £800,000 in new machinery which is to be paid out at once. There are two possible machines, which will produce the following cash inflows:

	Machine A £	Machine B £
Year 1	120,000	400,000
Year 2	150,000	400,000
Year 3	200,000	200,000
Year 4	380,000	150,000
Year 5	550,000	50,000

The firm's discount rate is 10%. Neither machine will have any residual value.

The payback period

This measures the length of time in which the cash inflows recover the initial investment.

For machine A, after four years the cash inflows total £850,000, so the project recovers its investment late in year 4. For machine B, the project recovers its investment at the end of year 2. Machine B pays back much earlier than machine A. Using this method, machine B would be a better investment.

A shorter payback period is regarded as safer because of the difficulties of being able to rely on forecasts for several years ahead. Machine B looks a better investment in that it is expected to bring in a total of £1.4 million, while machine B is only expected to bring in £1.2 million, but most of machine A's inflow is four and five years ahead.

However, the payback period method takes no account of the time value of money.

The accounting rate of return (ARR)

This method considers *profits* rather than cash flows. While there are many differences between profits and cash, the greatest difference is depreciation. Depreciation does not affect cash flow, but it does affect profits.

The ARR measures the average profits as a percentage of the investment.

As neither machine will have any residual value, the total depreciation in both cases is £800,000. The profits, therefore, are as follows:

	Machine A £	Machine B £
Total inflows	1,400,000	1,200,000
less depreciation	800,000	800,000
Total profits	600,000	400,000
Average over 5 years	120,000	80,000

The initial investment in both cases is £800,000, so the ARR is:

Machine A

$$\frac{\text{Average profits}}{\text{Initial investment}} \times 100 \qquad \frac{120,000}{800,000} \times 100 = 15\%$$

Machine B

$$\frac{\text{Average profits}}{\text{Initial investment}} \times 100 \qquad \frac{80,000}{800,000} \times 100 = 10\%$$

This shows machine A to be a better investment.

An alternative method of calculating the ARR uses the *average* investment rather than the initial figure. This is useful where the projects being compared have different residual values.

The accounting rate of return also takes no account of the time value of money.

The net present value method (NPV)

This method takes account of the fact that money values decrease over time. The amount of decrease depends on what the company could have done with that money if it had been invested elsewhere, but for simplicity it is easiest to imagine it as being like inflation – as time goes by, £1 will buy less and less.

There is a mathematical formula which can be used to calculate these reducing values, but there are also tables of values which can be used instead. A copy of such tables is found at the end of this chapter.

The example we are using states that the discount rate is 10%. The tables show that, at 10%, the value of £1 decreases as follows:

Year 1	0.909
Year 2	0.826
Year 3	0.751
Year 4	0.683
Year 5	0.621

These factors are applied to the cash flows in each year. This gives the present value of the future cash flows in *today's* terms, which will be less than the actual cash flows. The initial expenditure is taken as being in Year 0, i.e. at the start of the project. The discount factor in year 0 is 1.0000, as at that time £1 is worth £1. Outflows are shown in brackets.

So, for machine A, the calculation is as follows:

	Cash flows £	Discount factor	Present value £
Year 0	(800,000)	1.000	(800,000)
Year 1	120,000	0.909	119,999
Year 2	150,000	0.826	123,900
Year 3	200,000	0.751	150,200
Year 4	380,000	0.683	259,540
Year 5	550,000	0.621	341,550
	Total net present value		195,189

You can see that the large sum of £550,000 in year 5 is reduced to only £341,550 in today's terms, because £1 in five years' time will be worth only 62p. The net present value of the investment is £195,189.

For machine B, the calculation is as follows:

	Cash flows £	Discount factor	Present value £
Year 0	(800,000)	1.000	(800,000)
Year 1	400,000	0.909	363,600
Year 2	400,000	0.826	330,400
Year 3	200,000	0.751	150,200
Year 4	150,000	0.683	102,450
Year 5	50,000	0.621	31,050
	Total net present value		177,700

The NPV of machine B is £177,700. Therefore machine A is a more worthwhile investment.

Considering risk in investments

There are several ways in which the risk of investments can be minimized. One is to accept only those projects with a short payback period. Another is to use a larger discount rate than normal to ensure that any projects which might produce a negative net present value are rejected. A third way is to calculate the results using several different possible cash flows and profits for the same project. These can also be given different probability weightings.

Activity 53

Your company is considering replacing its IT equipment at a cost of £200,000 to be paid out at once. You are given the following figures over the next five years:

Year	Profits	Cash flows in
	£	£
1	35,000	55,000
2	55,000	75,000
3	90,000	95,000
4	60,000	80,000
5	40,000	50,000

Another project is under consideration which has a net present value of £23,450 and an accounting rate of return of 15%. Your company's cost of capital is 10%.

1 Draw up a list of possible costs and benefits of the proposed system.
2 Calculate three methods of investment and appraisal and discuss which project you would recommend, giving the reasons for your choice.

See Feedback section for answer to this activity.

Summary

Now that you have completed this chapter you should be able to calculate the financial effects of a range of short-term and long-term decisions, and consider various non-financial implications of such decisions.

DECISION MAKING

Review and discussion questions

1 What are the implications of accepting special orders when the firm is operating above break-even point, but below full capacity?
2 What are the implicatations of accepting special orders when the firm is operating at full capacity?
3 What might affect a decision to continue making a product even though it could be bought elsewhere for less?
4 Is it always advisable to cease making unprofitable products?
5 What are the three main methods of investment appraisal and what are their differences?

Case study

Walker and Harvey Limited manufacture three products. The annual demand is for 10,000 of each. Details of the three products are as follows:

	X	Y	Z
Selling price	£6	£10	£20
Variable costs	£4	£5	£8
Fixed costs	£5,000	£4,000	£3,000
Labour hours	2	3	4

There are only 70,000 labour hours available at the moment. Each product could be bought in from an outside supplier:

Product X	£5
Product Y	£6
Product Z	£10

Should one of the products be dropped from production, and if so, which one? Would you consider buying it in? What factors would you consider in making your decision?

Work-based assignment

B1.1
B1.2

Identify two decisions (one short-term, one long-term) at work which involve the introduction of, amendment to, or deletion of, a product or service. Determine the costs and revenues involved and prepare calculations to support your recommendation to proceed or abandon the items you have chosen.

RESOURCES MANAGEMENT

Feedback

Activity 1 You might include things such as:

- to increase the number of customers by five per cent
- to obtain contracts from schools
- to improve the changing room facilities
- to obtain funding from the Sports Council
- to increase occupancy of the sports hall by twenty per cent

Activity 3

	£
Opening stocks	14,000
Purchases	120,000
	134,000
Less Closing stocks	12,000
Cost of goods sold	122,000

Activity 4 **Lesley Biggs – Trading and profit and loss account for the year ended 31 December xxx1**

	£	£
Sales		180,000
less cost of goods sold		122,000
Gross profit		58,000
Motor expenses	18,000	
Printing, post, stationery	5,000	
Wages and salaries	24,000	
Depreciation	2,000	
		49,000
Net profit		9,000

Activity 5

(a) £30,000

(b) £60,000

Activity 6

Lesley Biggs – Balance sheet at 31 December xxx1

	£	£	£
Fixed assets			
Motor vehicles – cost		10,000	
– depreciation		2,000	
			8,000
Current assets			
Stocks	12,000		
Debtors	23,000		
Prepayments	500		
Bank	10,000		
		45,500	
less Current liabilities			
Creditors	8,000		
Accrued expenses	300		
		8,300	
			37,200
			45,200
less Long term liabilities – loan			5,000
			40,200
Financed by			
Opening capital			46,000
Net profit			9,000
			55,000
less drawings			14,800
			40,200

Activity 7

They are all cash flows out, except for the sale of fixed assets.

Activity 8

	£
Share capital	100,000
Share premium	200,000
Retained profits	450,000
	750,000

RESOURCES MANAGEMENT

Activity 9

You might have included some of the following in your answer:

(a) from subscriptions and donations
(b) from the local health authority, and from private consulting fees
(c) from government funds, and course fees paid by students
(d) from government funds and from the collection of rates

Activity 10

You might have answered as follows:

(a) standing order
(b) cash
(c) cheque
(d) credit card
(e) BACS transfer

Activity 11

Cash budget for the six months to 30 June xxx1

	Jan £	Feb £	March £	April £	May £	June £
Receipts						
Capital	23,000					
Sales – cash	200	200	400	400	600	600
Sales – credit		1,800	1,800	3,600	3,600	5,400
Total receipts	23,200	2,000	2,200	4,000	4,200	6,000
Payments						
Plant and machinery	10,000					
Motor vehicles	12,000					
Purchases	1,500	1,500	3,000		3,000	4,500
Rent	1,000			1,000		
Postage		100	100	200	200	300
Wages	700	700	700	700	700	700
Total payments	25,200	2,300	3,800	1,900	3,900	5,500
Opening balance	nil	(2,000)	(2,300)	(3,900)	(1,800)	(1,500)
Total receipts	23,200	2,000	2,200	4,000	4,200	6,000
	23,200	–	(100)	100	2,400	4,500
Total payments	25,200	2,300	3,800	1,900	3,900	5,500
Closing balance	(2,000)	(2,300)	(3,900)	(1,800)	(1,500)	(1,000)

Cash shortages could be managed by reducing the period of credit to customers and encouraging more of them to pay at once; the purchase of plant, etc. could be by hire purchase or even leased. The business has no excesses, but in the future it is likely to have – these should be invested.

FEEDBACK

Activity 12

On starting up, expansion, buying another business, merging with another business, ongoing expenditure (stocks, wages, running costs), repaying loans, purchase of fixed assets (shelving, freezers, storage areas), providing information systems and technology, paying redundancy costs.

Activity 14

You might have answered as follows:

(a) leasing or hire purchase
(b) mortgage
(c) bank overdraft
(d) government grants
(e) business angels

Activity 15

Gross profit margin	40%
Gross profit mark-up	$66\frac{2}{3}$%
Net profit margin	10%
Return on Capital Employed	5%

Activity 16

Current ratio	1.5:1
Acid test ratio	0.625:1

The ideal current ratio is 2:1, but many organizations manage with lower ratios, depending on the type of organization and its customers/suppliers. A ratio of 1.5:1 means that there is £1.50 in current assets to cover every £1 of current liabilities. The acid test ratio excluded stock from the calculation, assuming that it cannot be quickly converted into cash. An ideal ratio is 1:1. The above shows that there is only 62.5p in liquid assets for every £1 of current liabilities, which might cause liquidity problems.

Activity 17

Stock turnover	3.1 times per annum
Debtor days	30
Creditor days	39
Fixed asset turnover	£3

Activity 18

Gearing ratio	$33\frac{1}{3}$%
Earning per share	6.66p

Activity 19 You might have included many of the items mentioned in the text such as insurance, supervisors' wages, telephone charges, marketing etc., but some additional ones could be the cost of delivery vehicles, running the purchasing department, the managing director's car, secretarial support – even the work's canteen.

Activity 20

Item of expenditure	Materials, labour or expenses?	Direct or indirect?
Salaries of office staff	Labour	Indirect
Printing inks	Materials	Direct
Repairs to machinery	Expenses	Indirect
Printer's wage	Labour	Direct
Paper costs	Materials	Direct
Telephone costs	Expenses	Indirect
Fee to design artist	Labour	Direct
Insurance	Expenses	Indirect
Cleaning materials	Materials	Indirect
Rent and rates	Expenses	Indirect

Activity 21 Canteen costs per person = £18,000/60 employees = £300 per person.

Apportionment:

Sales and marketing	£4,200
Accounts	£2,400
Payroll	£1,200
Purchasing	£3,000
Research	£900
Production	£6,300

Activity 22

You might choose floor area for rent, volume of rooms for heating, cost or book value for equipment insurance, number of employees for the training department and health and safety costs, and number of terminals for the computer department costs.

If you chose something different, it may well be appropriate in some circumstances. Try to justify your choice – the textbook answer is not necessarily the best.

Activity 23

Overheads per productive hour = £1,500/120 hours = £12.50 per hour

Total job cost:

Direct costs 10 hours × £30	£300
Overheads 10 hours × £12.50	£125
Profit required	£200
Total price	£625

Activity 24

	Jan	Feb	March
Opening stock	300	400	600
Production	800	800	800
	1,100	1,200	1,400
Sales	700	600	650
Closing stock	400	600	750

It would seem that production is rather high for the current level of sales, resulting in a continual increase in closing stock. Whether this is acceptable or not depends on management policy as to the level of stock on hand.

Activity 25

	Jan	Feb	March
Materials	1,600	1,600	1,600
Labour	6,400	6,400	6,400
Overheads	2,400	2,400	2,400
Total production cost	10,400	10,400	10,400

Activity 26

	Budget £	Actual £	Variance £
Sales	60,000	64,000	4,000 F
Direct materials	28,000	30,000	2,000 A
Direct labour	12,000	11,500	500 F
Variable expenses	6,000	5,000	1,000 F
Fixed costs	8,000	8,600	600 A
Total costs	54,000	55,100	1,100 A
Profit	6,000	8,900	2,900 F

Activity 27

Assuming that the firm still makes 5,000 units, it would have expected to have used materials costing £15,000, so it has 'overspent' by £3,000. This could be because material was more expensive than planned – the 15,000 kg could have cost £1.20 per kg (which totals £18,000); or it could have used more than planned, say 18,000 kg at £1 per kg. It could even have used 20,000 kg at 90p per kg – a reduction in the price per kilogram, but a substantial increase in the quantity used. Other combinations of reasons are also possible.

Activity 28

	Revised budget £	Actual £	Variance £
Sales	62,500	70,000	7,500 F
Direct materials	25,000	26,000	1,000 A
Direct labour	20,000	18,000	2,000 F
Variable expenses	5,000	5,500	500 A
Fixed costs	5,000	4,500	500 F
Total costs	55,000	54,000	1,000 F
Profit	7,500	16,000	8,500 F

Activity 29

Manufacturing account for the year ending 30 September xxx1

	£000	£000
Raw materials:		
Opening stocks		6,700
Purchases	8,000	
Carriage inwards	150	
		8,150
		14,850
less closing stocks		4,600
Direct materials consumed		10,200
Direct labour		1,600
Power costs		1,300
Prime cost		13,100
Indirect factory expenses:		
Factory supervisors	5,200	
Factory rent	400	
Depreciation	300	
Heat and light	100	
Rates	800	
		6,800
Total Factory Cost of Production		19,900
Add: opening work in progress	3,600	
Less: closing work in progress	4,800	
		(1,200)
Factory cost of goods completed		18,700

Trading and profit and loss account for the year ending 30 September xxx1

	£000	£000
Sales		15,700
less cost of goods sold:		
Opening stocks of finished goods	7,100	
Factory cost of goods completed	18,780	
	25,880	
less closing stocks of finished goods	11,600	
		14,280
Gross profit		1,420
Less Expenses:		
Office salaries	100	
Rent	150	
Heat and light	150	
Depreciation	200	
Rates	200	
Delivery costs on sales	120	
General office expenses	180	
		1,100
Net profit		320

Activity 30

Cost statement for conference

Item	Units	Cost per unit £	Total cost £
Room hire	1	80	80
Lunch	44	35	1,540
Wines	20	8	160
Stationery	40	3	120
Projector hire	1	20	20
Overtime	4	100	400
Accommodation	44	50	2,200
Total cost			4,520

Activity 31

Revenue-earning departments might include rooms, restaurant, bar, leisure facilities, functions. Non-revenue earning departments might include reception, housekeeping and maintenance. There are lots of others too.

FEEDBACK

Activity 32

Operating statement for refectory – May

	Month £	Year to date £
Sales	18,000	78,000
Food	8,100	35,880
Gross profit	9,900	42,120
Wages	3,600	17,160
Gross operating profit	6,300	24,960
Other expenses	2,700	12,480
Net operating profit	3,600	12,480

Activity 33

Vehicle	A		B		C		D	
	Hours	%	Hours	%	Hours	%	Hours	%
Maximum usage	40	100.0	40	100.0	40	100.0	40	100.0
Actual usage	30	75.0	30	75.0	35	87.5	40	100.0
Breakdown time	5	12.5						
Idle time	5	12.5	10	25.0	5	12.5		

Activity 34

Overheads per hour = £10,000/400 = £25

Executive time = 20 hours x £45	£900
Materials	£350
Overheads = 20 hours × £25	£500
Total cost	£1,750
Profit required	£600
Selling price	£2,350

Activity 35

Yes, because it will bring in extra contribution:

Selling price	£20 per unit
Variable cost	£18 per unit
Revised contribution	£2 per unit

Additional contribution = 100 units × £2 each = £200

Thus extra profit of £200 will be made (or £200 less loss, if the organization has not yet sold enough to cover its fixed costs). Would you refuse £200 extra profit? Even if the fixed costs have not already been covered, extra contribution is worth having.

Activity 36

	£	£
Selling price		75,000
Variable costs:		
Direct materials	25,000	
Direct labour	20,000	
		45,000
Contribution		30,000
Fixed costs		15,000
Profit		15,000

Extra profit = contribution from 20 units.
Contribution per unit = £30,000/5,000 = £6
Extra profit = 20 × £6 = £120.

Variable costs = £9 per unit, so as £10 exceeds this the order should be accepted, provided that there is sufficient capacity and there are no other factors to consider.

Activity 37

Contribution per unit = £30,000/5,000 = £6.
Break even point   = fixed costs/contribution per unit
                      = £15,000/£6 = 2,500 units

Activity 38

	Flexed Budget	Actual Results	Variance
Sales value	230,000	253,000	23,000 F
Direct labour	27,600	23,000	4,600 F
Direct materials	110,400	128,800	18,400 A
Variable overheads	23,000	27,600	4,600 A
Fixed overheads	18,000	19,000	1,000 A
	179,000	198,400	19,400 A
Profit	51,000	54,600	3,600 F

Materials price variance = £110,400 − £147,200
                         = £36,800 Adverse

Materials usage variance = £147,200 − £128,800
                         = £18,400 Favourable.

Activity 39

(a) For the car, you might choose a supplier close by who offers after-sales service.

(b) For the computer installation, you might choose a supplier who provides advice and expertise.

(c) Supplier reputation might be most important for canteen supplies.

(d) Delivery arrangements might be important for raw materials.

Activity 40

You might choose cleaning services, laundry facilities, certain foods, alcoholic beverages.

Activity 41

You might consider some of the retailers such as Marks & Spencer, Boots the Chemist, or manufacturers.

Activity 42

	Small hotel with restaurant	Large hospital	Mobile take-away	Large international hotel
Fresh parsley for garnishing dishes	Local retailer	Contract	Local retailer	Contract
Fresh chicken portions	Market list	Contract	Cash and carry	Contract
Frozen beefburger	Market list/ cash and carry	Contract	Cash and carry	Central/contract
Liquid disinfectant	Cash and carry/ wholesaler	Contract	Cash and carry/ retailer	Central/contract
Serviettes	Cash and carry	Contract	Cash and carry	Central/contract
Potatoes	Market list	Contract	Cash and carry/ wholesaler	Market list/ central/contract

You can see that there is more than one possible choice for some.

Activity 43

ABC PRODUCTS LIMITED	PURCHASE ORDER
Broad Street New Town Manchester Telephone: 0161 821 9999	**NUMBER** 1234 **DATE:** 15 April xxx1 **To:** Burton and Harris plc Green Street, London

Description of Services	Qty	Price	Discount
A4 paper, 80 gsm Delivery in 10 days, f.o.c.	100 rms	2.40	10%
Authorised by:	*Jenny Smith*		

For details of the purpose of a purchase order, and how it should be used, refer back to page 155.

Activity 44

BURTON AND HARRIS PLC

Green Street
London
Tel: 0171 123 4567

To: ABC PRODUCTS LTD
Broad Street
New Town
Manchester

INVOICE No: 65718

Date 20 April xxx1

Del. note no.	Description of goods	Quantity	Price each	Total value
			£	£
B22	A4 paper, 80 gsm	100	2.16	216.00
		Total goods		216.00
		Plus VAT @ 17.5%		37.80
		Total invoice		253.80

For details of the purpose of an invoice, and how it should be used, refer back to pages 157–8.

Activity 45

FIFO

	Receipts			Issues			Balance		
	Qty	Value each	Total value	Qty	Value each	Total value	Qty	Value each	Total value
		£	£		£	£		£	£
April 1							100	10.00	1,000.00
April 8				24	10.00	240.00	76	10.00	760.00
April 18	38	12.00	456.00				38	12.00	456.00
April 20				50	10.00	500.00	26	10.00	260.00
April 23				26	10.00	260.00	38	12.00	456.00
				9	12.00	108.00	29	12.00	348.00
April 28	20	13.00	260.00				20	13.00	260.00
TOTALS	Receipts		716.00	Issues		1,108.00	Balance		608.00

LIFO

	Receipts			Issues			Balance		
	Qty	Value each	Total value	Qty	Value each	Total value	Qty	Value each	Total value
		£	£		£	£		£	£
April 1							100	10.00	1,000.00
April 8				24	10.00	240.00	76	10.00	760.00
April 18	38	12.00	456.00				38	12.00	456.00
April 20				38	12.00	456.00			
				12	10.00	120.00	64	10.00	640.00
April 23				35	10.00	350.00	29	10.00	290.00
April 28	20	13.00	260.00				20	13.00	260.00
TOTALS	Receipts		716.00	Issues		1,166.00	Balance		550.00

AVCO

	Receipts			Issues			Balance		
	Qty	Value each	Total value	Qty	Value each	Total value	Qty	Value each	Total value
		£	£		£	£		£	£
April 1							100	10.00	1,000.00
April 8				24	10.00	240.00	76	10.00	760.00
April 18	38	12.00	456.00				114	10.67	1,216.00
April 20				50	10.67	533.00	64	10.67	683.00
April 23				35	10.67	373.00	29	10.67	310.00
April 28	20	13.00	260.00				49	11.63	570.00
TOTALS	Receipts		716.00	Issues		1,146.00	Balance		570.00

Activity 46

Time based	– 40 hours at £3 per hour	£120.00
	– 5 hours at £4.50 per hour	£ 22.50
	Gross wages	£142.50
Output based	– 300 units at 25p	£ 75.00
	– 100 units at 50p	£ 50.00
	Gross wages	£125.00

Activity 47

Actual production $= 4,000/200$ hours $= 20$ per hour
Normal production $= 18$ per hour

Efficiency percentage $= 20/18 \times 100 = 111\%$

Activity 48

New order:
Contribution per unit = £40 − £30 = £10
Total additional contribution = £10 × 500 units = £5,000

Present orders:
Contribution per unit = £50 − £30 = £20
Break-even point = £40,000/£20 = 2,000 units

As break-even point has been reached, the new order will add £5,000 to profits. Providing that existing customers do not object to this, and that staff are available to work on the new order, it should be accepted.

Activity 49

Present contribution = £30 − £20 = £10 per unit
Total contribution = £10 × 2,000 units = £20,000
Current profit = contribution − fixed costs
= £20,000 − £12,000 = £8,000

Option 1 - buy in

Contribution per unit = £26 − £25
= £1 per unit × 200 units
= £200 extra profit

Option 2 - cut production

Contribution per unit = £26 − £20
= £6 per unit
Additional contribution of new order = £6 × 200 units
= £1,200
Lost contribution of existing orders = £10 × 200 units
= £2,000
= £800 less profit

Option 3 - expand

Additional contribution of new order = £6 × 200 units
= £1,200
less annual depreciation £500
= £700 extra profit

It would appear that Option 3 is the best, giving £700 extra profit. If the order is a one-off, however, and further new orders are not anticipated in the future, the annual depreciation charge will reduce future profits by £500 a year for 9 years.

Activity 50

At first sight, it seems better to buy in at £60, than to make at £65, but this depends on whether the fixed costs would still need to be paid. If they do, then the comparison should be between the cost of buying in and the *variable* cost of making:

Cost of buying in	£60
Variable cost of making	£45
Additional cost	£15

Therefore, it would not be wise to buy in.

Activity 51

	A £	B £	TOTAL £
Sales	4,000	6,000	10,000
Variable costs	2,000	2,000	4,000
Contribution	2,000	4,000	6,000
Fixed costs	2,250	2,250	4,500
Profit/(Loss)	(250)	1,750	1,500

The fixed costs have been apportioned equally between components A and B, so total profit actually falls by £1,000 due to the contribution lost from component C.

Activity 52

	A	B	C
Machine hours per unit	10	5	4
Machine hours required	20,000	15,000	16,000

Total 51,000 hours.

	A £	B £	C £
Selling price	30	40	50
Variable cost	5	25	30
Contribution per unit	25	15	20
Contribution per machine hour	£2.50	£3	£5

Cut production of product A.

	A	B	C
Production schedule – hours	17,000	15,000	16,000
– units	1,700	3,000	4,000
Shortfall	300		

Lost contribution from product A – 300 units × £25 = £7,500 less profit.

Activity 53

(a) Costs — equipment (hardware), programs (software), installation, development, training, disks, stationery, maintenance.

Benefits — greater speed and accuracy, larger volumes handled, less staff time, less storage space, greater flexibility, better reports, improved confidence and customer service.

(b) Payback period – towards the end of Year 3

Accounting rate of return
- profits £280,000 less depreciation of £200,000 = £80,000
- annual profits = £80,000/5 = £16,000
- average investment £100,000
- ARR = 16,000/100,000 × 100 = 16%

Net present value of future cash flows:

Year	Flow £	Factor £	Present value £
0	(200,000)	1	(200,000)
1	55,000	0.909	49,995
2	75,000	0.826	64,428
3	95,000	0.751	71,345
4	80,000	0.683	54,640
5	50,000	0.621	31,050
		Net present value	71,458

The project has a higher ARR than the alternative, and a greater net present value. Its payback period is relatively short, so it would seem a suitable investment.

Further reading

Bedward, D., Rexworthy, C., Blackman, C., Rothwell, A. and Weaver, M. (1997) *First Line Management*, Butterworth-Heinemann

Berry, A. (1993) *Financial Accounting*, Chapman and Hall

Broadbent, M. and Cullen, J. (1997) *Managing Financial Resources*, Butterworth-Heinemann

Lucey, T. (1993) *Costing*, DP Publications

Rickwood, C. and Thomas, A. (1992) *Introduction to Financial Accounting*, McGraw-Hill

Weaver, M. (1997) *Accounting*, Butterworth-Heinemann

Index